CHED EVANS

VINDICATED

To Ched Evans:
a victim of injustice, hypocrisy and much
else in human nature that is loathsome:
with sympathy for what he has endured.

And to his partner Natasha Massey and her father Karl Massey:
with great respect for the loving and steadfast support they gave
him through very difficult times.

Also to Dave Allen, Chairman of Chesterfield FC,
for having the courage to give Ched a new chance.

However some People may pretend, that unlawful Enjoyment is contrary to the Law of *Nature*; this is certain: that Nature never fails to furnish us largely with this Passion, tho' she is often sparing to bestow upon us such a Portion of Reason and Reflection as is necessary to curb it.

BERNARD MANDEVILLE

CHED EVANS

VINDICATED

against the Vile Aspersions cast upon him.

Essays criticising his Prosecution and Conviction, and deprecating the Odious Treatment to which he was subjected after leaving Prison.

J. Martin Stafford

Author of* The Prosecutor Unmask'd *etc.

With an Additional Essay
by Stuart Gilhooly.

Quid leges sine moribus vanae proficiunt? HORACE

ISMERON
SOLIHULL
2016

www.ismeron.co.uk

Printed and bound by

PMM Group Ltd., Garforth, LEEDS, LS25 2JY

A CIP catalogue record for this book is available from the British Library.

ISBN 978-0-9512594-7-4

Contents:

Preface

This little book has been long in gestation. Much of the material within its pages was conceived and written in the weeks immediately after Ched Evans's release from prison in mid-October 2014. A full account of how and why I became committed to his cause is given in the Introduction. Apart from a few refinements, expansions and additions, almost all had been drafted before Easter 2015. I then resolved that, whatever the outcome might be, I would publish my work as soon as the appeals processes to overturn his conviction were complete.

In the eighteen months between Evans's release from prison and the Court of Appeal's consideration of his case in the spring of 2016, I never envisaged that the Court would order a retrial – a decision that some may consider somewhat futile, given that Evans had already served the prescribed portion of his sentence. The petition by the Crown Prosecution Service that there should be a retrial if the conviction was overturned is quite consonant with the way in which now operates that vindictive and capricious institution, hardened in pride and insolence by its security from effective censure. I was ready to go to press in April 2016 and was also minded to do so. However, I was urged to postpone publication until such time as the case was fully resolved. By so doing, I have shown due respect for legal process and also enabled myself to comment on the final happy outcome. (See the Postscript on page 55.)

The phenomena with which I deal are the ugly offspring of moral laxity in low places and of folly and unscrupulous opportunism in higher ones. Like its predecessor, *The Prosecutor Unmask'd*, this tract includes more than one nod in the direction of Bernard Mandeville (1670-1733) – a perspicacious observer of human affairs and an arch-enemy of hypocrisy and self-deception. Throughout his active life, he took up his pen on numerous occasions to lampoon these frailties and the evils to which they give rise. For this reason alone, his books are well worth reading. Modern readers who peruse them (or the brief quotations from them included here) will recognise the world he described as the one that they live in. Those who are familiar with his best known work, *The Fable of the Bees*, will understand why I included a section in satirical verse, as this is an ideal medium in which to castigate vices and follies of all kinds; for ridicule can sometimes deliver a blow far more mortifying than mere refutation.

Like *The Fable of the Bees*, this book may be condemned by people who do not take the trouble to read it. Some will allege that it was written to excuse wrong-doing. Nothing could be further from the truth. I am no apologist for libertinism and licentiousness – as is eloquently testified by much of what I have published during my life. I thoroughly deplore the lubricious activities which led to the trial and conviction of Ched Evans; and he has himself expressed contrition for his part in them: a fact which – to their shame – his detractors refuse to acknowledge.

In recent decades we have raised at least one generation many of whom think it acceptable for human beings to romp about and copulate like rutting animals. I firmly maintain that in a culture which condones rampant promiscuity and does little to deter public drunkenness such incidents as led to the trial of Ched Evans are inevitable. Anyone who denies this is either a fool or a liar. The pervasive reluctance to be judgmental of casual sexual encounters and the tolerance of excessive drinking constitute an overwhelming twofold onslaught on moral restraint. It is acknowledged that alcohol, when consumed in quantity, diminishes our inhibitions. If these are weak to begin with, they will be very easily overcome. The baneful consequences are indeed inevitable.

Although to rid our streets of drunken, dissolute people would certainly be a step in the right direction inasmuch as it would forestall a great deal of mischief, a more effective remedy than any afforded by legislation or law-enforcement would be to inculcate dispositions conducive to chastity and sobriety. This truth was clearly enunciated in ancient times by the Roman poet Horace (65-8 BC) who asked, 'Of what avail are empty laws where there is great corruption of manners?' His words were quoted and endorsed twice by John Dennis in his now neglected book *Vice and Luxury Publick Mischiefs*.[1]

The pervasive disparagement of chastity is a particular symptom of a more general malaise: namely, the undervaluing of self-control. In his first book, Herbert Spencer remarked that by far the greatest cause of misery is lack of self-restraint.[2] I believe he was right. This certainly holds true in prosperous, civilized countries which enjoy political

---

[1] Horace: *Odes*, III.24.35-6. *Quid leges sine moribus vanae proficiunt?* Quoted by Dennis in *Vice and Luxury Publick Mischiefs*, 36 and 70-1.
[2] *Social Statics*, 353.

stability and where natural disasters – and acts of terrorism – are rare. The reasons why chastity and modesty evolved as 'artificial virtues'[3] are too complex to be adequately discussed in this short book. I would refer anyone curious enough to undertake further enquiries to the entries on David Hume (1711-76), Herbert Spencer (1820-1903), Edward Westermarck (1862-1939) and Roger Scruton (b.1944) that I contributed to Alan Soble's encyclopaedia *Sex from Plato to Paglia.*

I also note – with great concern and profound sadness – that, in a society where so many individuals and professions are tainted with self-serving dishonesty, the prosecution and subsequent scapegoating of Ched Evans were also virtually inevitable. The latter was facilitated by the stultifying tyranny of 'political correctness', stifling, as it does, the expression of heterodox opinion. The treatment meted out to Ched Evans has further demeaned and disfigured a society which was already in a state of serious moral crisis.

If people dislike what I have written, they should subject my work to the most rigorous examination and analysis. I am fairly confident that they will find only one thing wrong with what I say: namely, that it is true. I have an unbroken record over more than four decades of not being successfully controverted in print. The censures I deliver in the ensuing pages are hard-hitting: but I should be both surprised and sorry if it could be shown that I have said anything that is untrue or treated any person or corporate body unfairly. It was certainly never my intention to do so.

I acknowledge my gratitude to the following for their encouragement in undertaking this literary project: the veteran Mandeville scholar Irwin Primer, Emeritus Professor of Rutgers University, New Jersey; Ned Boagni, now of Lyon, France; Paul Temperton; Stephen Willis; and Stuart Hulley. Had he still been alive, Allan Horsfall (1927-2012), whom I knew for over forty-five years, would also have supported me. I am, of course, especially indebted to Stuart Gilhooly for permission – very willingly granted – to include his work alongside my own.

J. Martin Stafford

15 October 2016

---

[3] This term was deployed by David Hume in Book III of *A Treatise of Human Nature* to denote those virtues that 'arise from education, from the voluntary conventions of men, and from the interest of society'. See 3.2.12 'Of Chastity and Modesty', *Treatise*, 364-6.

1. Introduction

Before the middle of October 2014 I knew nothing of Ched Evans. I might have heard his name, but it meant nothing to me. A few days before his release from prison, I saw reports of an on-line petition to blight his hopes of reinstatement at Sheffield United F.C. After voicing the most tentative opposition to this objective, the broadcaster Judy Finnigan suffered a tirade of vituperative abuse, and her daughter was threatened. Although the threats were very probably empty ones, the abuse was real enough. I found this sinister and alarming. Unlike much that is reported in the papers, the issues surrounding this case are a matter of serious public interest. I contend that people must feel free to express their opinions, however controversial, without intimidation. As in every area of inquiry, their views should be subject to rigorous examination and open to challenge.

I decided to look into the matter. I have no interest in football and am not (or rather I *was* not) one of Ched Evans's fans. I therefore approached the circumstances in which he was convicted with impartial detachment. Having looked at the facts, I found his conviction deeply disturbing. The person who shared the dock with him on the same charges was acquitted at the same time as Evans was convicted, although there seemed to be little significant difference in the evidence against them, and certainly not such as to warrant the disparity in the outcome. I was at a loss to understand why the jury reached different verdicts – an incomprehension which I did not know at the time was shared by at least one other person perhaps better qualified than I to have an opinion in the matter.[1] Three significant people were voluntarily

---

[1] The Irish lawyer, Stuart Gilhooly, solicitor to the Irish Professional Footballers' Association and a respected journalist, wrote a trenchant piece questioning the 'guilty' verdict and defending, in any event, Evans's right to return to football. It was posted on the Irish PFA website on 17 November, 2014. It was up for only a few hours, as

present at the 'crime scene'. All were up to no good. From a moral point of view, there seemed little difference between them. One walked away unpunished, but not untainted; one received the much-prized accolade of victimhood;[2] and one was branded a vicious rapist. I found this outcome morally repugnant and an affront to common sense.

Evans has freely admitted that on the night in question he behaved very badly, but has consistently – and in my view convincingly – protested his innocence of the crime of rape. He has been unfailingly supported in this not only by his own family but also by his partner, Natasha Massey and her father, Karl. To my mind, this speaks volumes. I know men who have daughters recently married or of marriageable age. Any father has a powerful instinct to protect his daughter from the attentions of the sort of man that Ched Evans has been cast as. Mr Massey has demonstrated his whole-hearted support for Ched, despite his conviction and the sordid events that led to it. Moreover, it was Mr Massey who

---

various women's groups – determined to stifle the expression of opinions that conflict with their own – exerted pressure on the Irish PFA to remove it. The Irish PFA, reluctant to court bad publicity and recognising that this battle was not theirs to fight, acceded to these demands. The proprietor of Ismeron is made of sterner stuff, and so the text is reproduced as an additional chapter to this book. See pages 42-47 below.

[2] This particular girl's status as a 'victim' has hardly proved to be a blessing to her; nor, since she expressly disclaimed all recollection of the alleged offence, is it something that she sought but rather something that was foisted on her by the CPS's decision to prosecute, the subsequent conviction and the determination of feminist groups to proclaim and exploit her status as such. During Evans's imprisonment and also after his release, she was hounded and harassed by some of his more ardent sympathisers, who were naturally indignant at his conviction and further antagonised by the unconscionable treatment meted out to him after he left prison. Many believe that had Evans been allowed promptly to resume his career with Sheffield United, much of this acrimony and resentment would have abated, and that this stupid, unlucky girl would then have suffered no more hostile attention. While counterfactual speculation cannot, by its very nature, be supported by evidence, this is a view that I whole-heartedly endorse.

funded the appeal against conviction and has resolutely stood by Ched in his fight to regain his career. I have never believed that Ched Evans is a rapist, and so I too am committed to supporting him. I think he was a silly young man, who in a moment of drunken stupidity allowed his very worst impulses to get the better of him. This is a weakness he has in common with many of his profession and even more outside it.[3] I suspect that if all professional footballers who have ever engaged in casual sexual activity with loose, drunken women were debarred from the game, there would be very few matches played; for many clubs would be hard-pressed to field a team.

The second reason why I support him is that, even if he had been guilty, he was duly punished. There is a long-established and widely respected principle that after serving a period in prison, people should, wherever possible, be reinstated to their place in society and fully rehabilitated. In Evans's case this principle was grossly violated without sufficient reason. One reason advanced was that, as a professional footballer, he serves as a role model. This is a specious but spurious argument. In a radio programme in which his case was discussed,[4] the *Sunday Times* sports correspondent, David Walsh, made the telling point that many professional sportsmen are very *bad* role models. Why should we expect otherwise? A few moments' thought should convince us that good and bad patterns of conduct are to be found in people from all walks of life and even from the same persons at different times. Wherefore the need to cultivate in ourselves and to foster in others a discerning moral sensitivity which will not follow slavishly the examples of any particular individuals. Another contributor to this programme, Claire Fox, pointed out that football, like other sports, is a game, not a demonstration of morality. Since then, the Irish journalist Brian O'Connor has

---

[3] As Bernard Mandeville observed: "Nature never fails to furnish us largely with this Passion, tho' she is often sparing to bestow upon us such a Portion of Reason and Reflexion as is necessary to curb it". (*Public Stews*,7)

[4] BBC Radio 4 *The Moral Maze*, 22 October 2014.

confronted head-on the facile assumption that young people uncritically adopt sportsmen as role models.

> The idea that sports stars should be role models is a childish conceit possessed solely by adults. No child is silly enough to think because someone is good at kicking a ball or running fast they should also be pillars of humanism. Only adults can manage to be that wilfully dumb.[5]

A similar point is made by Luke Gittos, commenting on the implacable hostility to Evans's restoration to a footballing career.

> Time and time again, commentators emphasised that allowing Evans to play would lead to him being seen as a 'role model' among young people, who would come to idolise him both for his footballing ability and for his sexual violence [*sic*]. When I heard this argument...I would ask what these people thought of the parents of the young people they were talking about. Did they have no role in influencing what aspect of Evans their children came to respect?[6]

Moreover, it was hardly as if Ched Evans was presenting himself to the public as an unrepentant rapist, and maintaining that this is acceptable. Rather, he contended that he had been falsely accused and wrongly convicted of rape, and that he sought to redress this. The distinction between these two diametrically opposite standpoints and the very different practical implications that they entail should always have been taken into account. Until his arrest, his career had been untainted by scandal or disgrace. He was a very popular and well respected member of his team. It is both unfair and unrealistic to require someone of Evans's age and immaturity to be a *moral* role model. Given the chance, he may have remarkable potential for this, since he acknowledges that he acted badly, claims to have learned from his mistakes, and resolves not to make similar ones in the future. Only time will tell.

---

[5] *Irish Times*, 12 January 2015.

[6] Luke Gittos: *Why Rape Culture is a Dangerous Myth*, 95.This author is wrong to allege that Evans was guilty of violence. There was no evidence to suggest that he or his co-defendant deployed force or violence of any kind whatsoever. This book is discussed on pages 58-60 below.

My third reason for supporting Evans is that I think he has been used as a scapegoat. His exploitation in this capacity has been not only connived at but actively encouraged by prominent politicians and at least one churchman. I deplore such conduct in people who, as appointed leaders and guardians of public standards, are paid to know better than to promote the dangerous illusion that by making scapegoats of particular persons we can cure the ills that afflict us. In my submission, anyone who lacks the sense to see this or the candour to acknowledge it is unfit to hold any public office.

At the time of his release from prison, much of the animosity against Evans was fuelled by an on-line petition. Those who drafted and subscribed to it have justifiable grievances about the abuse suffered by women; but they chose a very bad site on which to fight their battle. Here there was no moral high ground on which they could take a firm stand. Here there was no black and white: only shades of grey – and very dirty grey at that. The 'victim' was not a victim in any serious sense of the word, as her experience on that night was a predictable consequence of the bad choices that she herself had freely made. Call this 'victim-blaming' if you so choose. I call it a warrantable censure of reckless and indecent behaviour. Moreover, Evans's status as a 'rapist' was always far too dubious to make him a convincing villain. These words were labels, attached for polemical convenience, but they were never an accurate description of the underlying reality. The authors of such petitions and all their fellow-travellers need to take full account of the dark cultural complexities which have led to the pervasive moral deficiencies that rightly concern them but which most of them seem to have neither the intelligence to grasp nor the courage to confront.

Having resolved to stand by Ched Evans in his attempts both to overturn his conviction and to be restored to professional football, I sought the moral support of a handful of people. On so controversial a matter, I did not want to take a solitary public stand if I could avoid doing so. Three were academics who I thought might be sympathetic to the cause. I also approached two diocesan bishops: St Asaph (where Ched was born and raised) and Sheffield (where his career had blossomed). It was with a degree of mild apprehension that I approached one of the academics – the distinguished philosopher Roger Scruton – as I had criticised (though always respectfully) one particular aspect of his work in the pages of academic journals and in an entry on him that I wrote for an encyclopaedia.[7] Of the five that I approached, he was the only one to respond positively; and he did this within hours of my appeal. One of the academics declined to help me and one did not respond at all. This calls to mind a story in the Bible in which aid was forthcoming from the least expected quarter.[8] The irony of this is not lost on me, and I hope it will not be lost on my readers.

I found the response of the two bishops very disappointing indeed – a reaction which may be indicative of my own naivety. Evidently, elevation to episcopal rank in the established church may come at the price of enthrallment to other features of 'The Establishment'. They were too complacent and too self-righteous by far for my liking. Since the Christian religion waxes so lyrical about second chances, forgiveness and redemption; and since its founder was unjustly sentenced to death, I expected a more questioning attitude to judicial processes and a more magnanimous one towards someone who claimed – with good reason – to be a victim of injustice. Readers may judge for themselves by perusing the text of the emails exchanged.

To the Bishops of Sheffield and St Asaph: re. Ched Evans.

Right Reverend Sirs,

In the last three weeks, my mind has been greatly exercised by this case. Late last week I composed the attached piece [a document that makes more or less *verbatim* all the points contained in the first seven paragraphs of this Introduction], which states my thoughts clearly and succinctly. I am seeking to have it published

---

[7] 'Love and Lust Revisited: Intentionality, Homosexuality and Moral Education'; 'The Two Minds of Roger Scruton'; and the entry in Alan Soble's encyclopaedia *Sex from Plato to Paglia*.

[8] 'The Parable of the Good Samaritan', *Luke* x, 30-7.

and have sought the help of the Professional Footballers' Association. I am acquainting you with my thoughts as Ched was born in St Asaph and worked in Sheffield. I do this partly as a courtesy to you, but also because I should be grateful for your support. I should like a few people to subscribe to a paragraph saying that they share my concerns and are broadly in agreement with what I say. I have not asked many people. So far I have secured the support of one person: the distinguished philosopher, Roger Scruton. I am familiar with his work as I wrote the entry on him for an encyclopaedia. I shall not think ill of you if you decline to support me.

Yours sincerely,

J. Martin Stafford (3 November 2014)

Dear Mr Stafford,

Thank you for your email and reflections. I was honoured to serve as a magistrate for six years, and in that time I learned to distrust the reporting of any trial, but to accept that the courts system is thorough and cases are tested by prosecution and defence. Although there are miscarriages of justice, caused by corruption or contamination or manipulation of the evidence, on the whole, those who are judge and jury have a far better sense of the rights and wrongs of the case than those who only hear reports. I am not therefore willing to challenge the finding of the court in this case, and accept its verdict that Ched Evans is a convicted rapist. If there has been a miscarriage of justice in this case, then those who know better than I must make their case.

However, while Ched Evans is a convicted rapist, I think that to restore him to the position of a professional footballer and thereby as a role model and hero for young people would send out entirely the wrong signals. When a person serves their time, they are entitled to a new beginning, and even, in the Christian faith, forgiveness, but neither of these things imply restoration to the *status quo ante.*[9]

I regret that I cannot support your text.
Yours sincerely,
+Gregory Llanelwy
[Rt. Rev. Dr. Gregory Cameron, Bishop of St Asaph, 4 November]

Thank you for your message Martin.

My views on the matter are similar to those of the Bishop of St Asaph and I cannot offer my support in this instance.

With kind regards.

Steven [Rt. Rev. Steven Croft, Bishop of Sheffield, 6 November]

In the many long months since I drafted my email to these two latter-day Pharisees,[10] my attitude has hardened considerably, and I must admit that I now view them with some aversion. If they find that my strictures make for uncomfortable reading, they have only themselves to blame. In the course of my own life I have usually made wise choices, from which I have reaped the anticipated benefits. This might sometimes have caused *me* to be complacent and self-righteous. But were I to enter the lists for a prize for self-righteousness, then in a field where I was faced with such formidable competition as they present, I should be very poorly placed indeed: merely an 'also-ran'!

[9] *status quo ante* (a Latin expression) = how things stood before.
[10] The Pharisees were a Jewish religious party distinctly identified as such in the second century BC. Their interpretation of Judaism was rigorously legalistic, and they remonstrated with Christ for consorting with sinners and forgiving their sins. He, in turn, repeatedly denounced them. See *Matthew* xxii, 13-26 and *Luke* xviii, 9-14. See also the entry 'Pharisees' in *The Oxford Dictionary of the Christian Church*, p.1059.

Apart from a letter published in the *Oldham Evening Chronicle* on 16 January 2015,[11] the public stance I hoped to take in defence of Ched Evans has not been manifested until now, though this was not for want of trying on my part. My approaches to the media met with a poor response. I attribute this to their general hostility to the cause I espouse[12] and to my non-demotic style of writing, which, in a world of shallowness and superficiality, many might find alien and off-putting. I am not a man of ten second soundbites or terse one-liners. To treat so serious a subject as this in so perfunctory a manner would, in my view, be irresponsible and discourteous to all parties. Anyone who has read thus far will have perused a dozen meticulously constructed paragraphs in which facts are clearly presented and cogent arguments adduced. My style has been developed over forty-odd years to meet the once exacting standards of scholarly journals. It has served me well, and I have no mind to change it now.

However, to indulge my own whimsy and by way of light relief, I *do* present my readers with an account of the principal incidents in the Ched Evans saga in satirical verse. This serves both to present a summary of the story and to lampoon those hostile forces which have ranged themselves against him. If any Celtic bard is inspired to translate my verses into Welsh, permission will readily be granted for this project.

---

[11] Reprinted on page 37.

[12] See Note 3, p. 31.

2. The Persecution of Ched Evans

***A MORAL SATIRE** wherein the principal elements of the story are recounted in an easy and familiar manner, fit to instruct and entertain people of all capacities.*

I. EXORDIUM

When silly youngsters have too much to drink,
Into disorder they are prone to sink.
The more so if they've been raised at a time
When fornicating's thought to be no crime,
And many do not worry in the least
If boy or girl acts like a rutting beast.
Nor can we cultivate propriety,
When we encourage insobriety.
I now recount the wryest of strange tales:
A tale of woe that started in North Wales.

II. RHYL

One night a sporting Welshman and his friend
Into the town of Rhyl their way did wend.
And on that night a girl was on the prowl,
Her head full of intentions lewd and foul.
In the small hours, while wandering on a street,
She with Ched's friend McDonald by chance did meet.
They went by taxi to a Premier Inn.
She more than he was well intent on sin.
No girl of easy virtue more content
To drop her knickers and, with full assent,
Throw caution to the wind and raid the store
Of Venus's sensual pleasures to take more.

She knew not then that, in her quest for fun,
She would have two, all for the price of one.
Before with her McDonald had had his fill
He thought that she'd be well up for it still.
A text message he then sent to young Ched,
Inviting him to mount their gruesome bed.
And he, responding to th' enticing text,
Was so ill-fated as to have her next.

Now on the morrow this unruly miss
Lay naked on the bed in her own piss:
No recollection of the night before;
Unmindful that she'd played the willing *****.
All came to light because the hapless ****
Told the Police that she had lost her bag.
In the investigation that ensued
The young footballers both were interviewed.
Th' ingenuous lads admitted to the fact
That each with her had known a carnal act –
But by consent! She had with each agreed
To gratify a sordid, bestial need.
To slake the lust that set their loins afire
This wanton trio gladly did conspire.
No sign of force, of injury or constraint,
Of aught that could give rise to a complaint.

III. FIRST TRIAL & APPEAL

We reason soundly but from what we know;[13]
This case to trial was never fit to go.
No certain facts that could support belief;
And yet the Law was bent on bringing grief.

---

[13] Cf. Alexander Pope: *Essay on Man* I.18.

After ***eight weeks*** both men were charged with rape.
I tell you truly: this is not a jape.
In Britain's new-found pseudo-puritan age
Are hypocrites, eager to vent their rage;
Vile opportunists – keen to make their mark –
Who act from motives sinister and dark;
And scapegoat-seekers, anxious to deflect
Attention from themselves, so imperfect.

The case the Prosecution would present
Was that she'd been too drunk to give consent.
But what none ever thought would come to be:
One was found guilty; t'other was set free.
Verdict perverse! Too crazy, too insane
Credit with any but lunatics to gain.
If she had been too drunk to shag with Ched,
Then likewise with the other on that bed.

The bigwigs on their high judicial bench
Were resolute the processes to wrench;
And, for to make a wayward verdict fit,
Now forced all better reasoning to submit.
Thus they were most peremptorily insistent
That in this case there was naught inconsistent.
So Ched, by such a devious trial dejected,
Found that this first appeal was fast rejected.[14]

IV. SHEFFIELD

To Ched in prison Blades[15] officials came,
Assuring his restoration to the game.

---

[14] This stanza refers to the refusal by the Court of Appeal on 6 Nov. 2012 to grant leave to appeal against conviction. See Note 2, pp. 29-31.

[15] The local name for Sheffield United Football Club, derived from the city's history as a centre for the production of cutlery, scissors, etc.

"When, in due course, you're free to show your face
Once more at Bramall Lane you'll have a place."
Alas! Jean Hatchet's on vindictive mission
With her mendacious, mean on-line petition;
Determined downcast Ched's career to blight,
Hoping his fans cannot put up a fight.
More hostile forces to the fray resort:
Minor celebrities, who all count for naught.

Then from Olympian heights, bedecked in gold,
An awesome goddess made our blood run cold.
Miss Longlegs[16] said her name must be removed
If Ched's return to Sheffield was approved.
So promises that had so oft been spoken
Were now as pie crusts: made but to be broken;
As by the team for which so well he'd played
Ched was at last abandoned and betrayed.
We've seen disgrace in politicians, bankers:
Ne'er such a shower of abject, spineless *******.

V. OLDHAM

The New Year soon got off to a fair start
With news to gladden and uplift our heart.
Oldham Athletic wished to take him on
In spite of what he did – or might have done.
But now so thoroughly demonized was Ched
That all and sundry took it in their head
To rail and fulminate against the lad –
An unrepentant rapist! – Far too bad
Ever again to play for any team.
Police and Crime Commissioner did deem
That he had never shown the least remorse
Or token of regret. And, what is worse,

[16] Olympic gold medallist, Jessica Ennis-Hill.

The local bishop promptly did inveigh
That on their pitch he was unfit to play.

This MONSTROUS LIE that Ched showed no contrition
Encountered very little opposition.
The tabloid press has made for many years
A fortune out of other people's tears;
And by the lies they print do propagate
Unfounded animosity and hate.
But I know better than to think such things.
I saw the video he made, which brings
Me all th' assurance I could ever need
To know he's sorry for his errant deed.
And, what is more, his partner and her dad
Stand resolutely by this contrite lad.
Ochlocracy's vile force[17] did now prevail,
Which all right-thinking people must bewail;
And on the fifth day that so soon did dawn
The offer to recruit him was withdrawn.

VI. THE MORAL

I preach this moral to all girls and boys:
Be more restrained in tasting carnal joys.
To take such pleasure without love's sweet throes
Means little more than when you blow your nose.
When feeling randy, do not take a chance:
Hold up your knickers; keep dicks in your pants.
The Prosecutor may be lurking nigh,
Or furtive minions, who on you may spy.
All are intent on getting a conviction
E'en though the case against you be a fiction.

---

[17] ochlocracy = mob rule.

3. A Catalogue of Woes

Given my censorious temperament, I am probably among the last people who would be a natural candidate to support Ched Evans, but support him I do – with all the energy and skill I can muster. Accounts of the events in the hotel room near Rhyl which led to his conviction make for unedifying reading. But of one thing I am fully assured: on that fateful night there was no 'victim' in any ordinary or serious sense of the word. Though what took place was lewd and sordid, no rape was committed. The three who participated in sexual activity (Evans, McDonald and the unnamed girl) as well as their voyeuristic entourage were all present of their own volition and were willing – perhaps even eager – spectators or participants in what took place.

The law on rape surely needs to be far more sensitive to the nuances of different circumstances. A clear distinction should be drawn between those who are rapists by predatory design and those who are 'rapists' by accident. The former would – paradigmatically – include men who prowl around with masks over their faces and knives in their hands, intent on violating whoever might come across their path. A drunken man who engages in consensual activity with a woman who also has had too much to drink is surely not in quite the same category. Those self-appointed champions of women's rights who deny this, constantly mouthing the facile and deceitful slogan '***Rape is rape***', do a grave disservice to a cause that in many respects is legitimate. It is high time they had the sense to see the error of their ways. Their refusal to do so is, of course, due to the fact that the most zealous of them are disciples of Catherine MacKinnon (b.1946). She maintains that, by reason of the economic relationship between the two sexes, *all* sexual activity between men and women is tantamount to rape. Accordingly, their agenda, whether hidden or declared, is not to refine distinctions between categories but to conflate them.[18]

---

[18] See Note 1 'The Influence of Catherine MacKinnon', p. 26 below.

In mitigation of Evans's misconduct, it can be pleaded with much plausibility that what happened on that night is symptomatic of a more pervasive and deep-rooted malaise. I am forty years older than he is. Within my adult lifetime, many of the social conventions which once imposed restrictions on the libidinous propensities of young people have been eroded and undermined – arguably with dire consequences.[19] Evans and others of his generation have grown up in a culture in which excessive drinking and sexual promiscuity are rife, and regarded by many as acceptable. Accordingly, we have no reason to be surprised – and very little right to feel indignant – when such incidents take place. They are the inevitable result of a moral decline that many have connived at. Evans has had the grave misfortune to be an easy and convenient scapegoat for ills for which he is only minimally responsible. He has been unscrupulously used as such by those who are uncomfortable with the evils brought about by our increasingly amoral society but have neither the sense to identify nor the courage to denounce the root causes.

1. Opportunism

Given that the girl disclaimed all recollection of what happened and had sustained no injuries of any kind, why were the two young men charged with rape? And why was there a time lapse of two months between their arrest and the decision to charge them? The answer to these questions is straightforward enough, but profoundly disconcerting; for it suggests that Evans was a victim of opportunism. The Crown Prosecution Service – like the National Health Service and many educational institutions – has become 'target-driven'. This culture can be corrupting, and at

---

[19] The most significant influence on this process was probably the advent in the early 1960s of the contraceptive pill. This was complemented in 1967 by legislation in England and Wales which led to abortion being available virtually on demand. As these two developments tended to annihilate the risk of unwanted pregnancy, they gave women a freedom to behave promiscuously hitherto enjoyed only by men. Some women have made full use of this freedom, and so a once potent restraint on sexual licence has been eliminated.

times is deeply so. For instance, in some schools, useful subjects are dropped from the curriculum because they do not contribute to a rating in 'league tables'. In hospitals, statistics may be 'massaged' to make particular departments or whole institutions seem better-performing than they really are. We often hear complaints from feminist pressure groups and the politicians who creep to their humour that far too few men are charged with rape and even fewer convicted. This is an obstreperous catch-cry of the age. Given that both Evans and his companion had freely admitted to having intercourse (a fact which of itself indicates that they did not believe that they had done anything criminal) and given his burgeoning reputation as a Sheffield United and Welsh International striker, the CPS no doubt scented blood. Easy meat. The Crown might not secure a conviction, but the occupation of the defendants and the nature of the charges ensured that at least it would put on a mouth-watering show – and, though they did not know this at the time, one that would enjoy a revival when it was restaged in Cardiff four and a half years later.[20]

2. Injustice

What no one expected – and no wise person would have wanted – was the perverse outcome of the first trial's disparate verdicts: for while Evans was convicted of rape on the grounds that the girl was too drunk to have the capacity to consent, his co-defendant was acquitted. This is very hard indeed to understand.[21] These conflicting verdicts would have been justified only if there had been good reason to believe that the girl was more intoxicated when she was engaged with Evans than when she was with his friend. There was no evidence to support this conclusion. It was logically untenable, and therefore, to a well-ordered mind, psychologically unbearable. Evans must therefore have been the victim of a miscarriage of justice. The Irish lawyer, Stuart Gilhooly, has called the result 'bizarre', as well as suggesting that

[20] The regrettable consequences of the target-driven culture of the CPS are exposed and discussed by Luke Gittos in his provocative book *Why Rape Culture is a Dangerous Myth*. pp. 18, 30-32, 62-3.

[21] See Note 2 'The Perversity of the Disparate Verdicts', p. 29 below.

no case where the evidence was so tenuous would ever have seen the light of day in an Irish court.[22]

This Caernarvon trial was distinguished by another extraordinary event. Evans's parents aver that after their son had been sentenced the prosecuting barrister, John Philpotts QC, approached them and said, 'I'm so sorry!' Why did he do this? Perhaps it was the triumph of personal decency over professional posturing. If he had truly believed that he had just secured the conviction of a rapist, he would have had nothing whatsoever to be sorry about. If, on the other hand, his confident addresses to the jury concealed grave misgivings that he privately entertained; and if he realised that he had just participated in a grotesque charade – a travesty of justice that was responsible for sending an innocent young man to prison – then he had every reason to feel profoundly uneasy, knowing that he had just done the Devil's work.[23]

An outcome as controversial as this one must tend to bring the administration of justice into disrepute. The only possible public benefit that could be claimed is that Evans's conviction, however unsafe, might deter other men from reckless sexual conduct. This alleged benefit is nebulous, uncertain and – most seriously of all –

---

[22] Stuart Gilhooly's article is printed in full below, pp. 42-7.

[23] The theatricality of court proceedings and the duplicity of barristers are discussed in the Second Dialogue of *The Prosecutor Unmask'd*, where Philo says: "Although witnesses are on oath, barristers are not. Their role is to present one side of the case and to conceal any weaknesses as artfully as they can. […] To buoy up a poor case, barristers must sometimes say things that they do not sincerely believe, or at least they must claim to believe things with a degree of assurance that no reasonable person would feel." (16). Lawyers were among the many professions that Mandeville lampooned as self-serving and sometimes corrupt. In *The Fable of the Bees* he castigated those…

[Who] to defend a wicked Cause,
Examin'd and survey'd the Laws,
As Burglars Shops and Houses do,
To find out where they'd best break through. (*Fable*, Vol. I, p. 20).

was always morally tainted by the dubiety of Evans's guilt. The harm occasioned by this prosecution is indisputable. The careers and reputations of both the co-defendants were damaged. The girl also suffered greatly: not as a result of the events of the night in question but from the decision to prosecute, the ensuing trial, and its aftermath. Without the prosecution, it would probably have been for her just another in a series of casual sexual encounters: soon over and just as quickly forgotten.

Be it noted that in our own contemporary culture in contexts such as this one, the irresponsible conduct of women must *never* be reprehended or even challenged. Women must feel free to rake about the streets late at night, much the worse for drink, scantily dressed and deporting themselves shamelessly. But on no account should such factors ever be invoked as an explanation of the misfortunes that befall them. It is only men who are to be held accountable for acts of predation or opportunism.

In stark contrast to this moral prejudice now so well established here, societies subject to Islamic influence are still inclined to lay the preponderance of responsibility for sexual misconduct on women. They are the great temptresses, and so they must bear most of the blame.[24] I mention this striking disparity in cultural attitudes to highlight the injustice and folly of both extremes. This subject affords much food for thought, albeit unpalatable to many. Let us hope that this is an instance of a phenomenon noted by Herbert Spencer: namely that "the suppression of every error is commonly followed by a temporary ascendency of the contrary one",[25] and that one day there will be established an equitable mean in which men and women are held equally accountable for their venereal misdemeanours.

---

[24] Though this prejudice against women may survive in Islam, it also has deep roots in male-dominated Judeo-Christian tradition, according to which it was the very first woman, Eve, who introduced sin into the world by contravening God's explicit prohibition against eating the fruit of the tree of knowledge and tempting the first man, Adam, to join her. (*Genesis*, Chapter iii).

[25] *Education: Intellectual, Moral, and Physical*, p. 60.

3. Ignorance and Duplicity

Six months before his release from prison, Sheffield United's Team Manager, Nigel Clough, and the club's co-owner, Kevin McCabe, visited Evans to discuss the terms of his reinstatement. Clearly, this is what the club intended. Two earlier managers had made the same trip with the same message. All interested parties had been assured that, after serving the prescribed portion of his five-year sentence, Evans would be able to resume his career and get his life back on track. Such a step would have been in perfect accord with the way in which other professional footballers have been rehabilitated after criminal convictions. The most notable recent instance is that of Luke McCormick, who, after serving time for causing the death of two children by drunken driving, was allowed to resume his career with Plymouth Argyle, of which he became the captain. Here guilt was undisputed and the crime had fatal consequences; and yet a line was drawn under it.

In the very same month as it was revealed that SUFC intended to reinstate Evans, an on-line petition was launched to blight his hopes of a prompt return to football. The wording of the petition was flagrantly disingenuous and blatantly misleading, omitting to reveal the controversial circumstances of the conviction and the fact that Evans vehemently protested his innocence. At the same time, it introduced phrases which were not merely exaggerated but, in relation to this case, downright false: *gross acts of violence, atrocious crimes*. There was not a vestige of evidence, verbal or forensic, that Evans or his co-defendant had deployed force of any kind. The petition was deliberately contrived to deceive the unwary by creating the impression that the 'offence' was as serious as it could possibly be. It was – to echo apposite words once used elsewhere – *a practice very contrary to all rules of candour and fair-dealing, and a strong instance of those polemical artifices, which a bigoted zeal thinks itself authorized to employ.*[26]

---

[26] This quotation comes from the advertisement prefixed to the 1777 edition of David Hume's *Essays and Treatises on Several Subjects*. See his *Enquiries…*, p.2.

Its promoter masquerades under the pseudonym of 'Jean Hatchet'. Her aim – pursued with splenetic fanaticism and little regard for the truth – was to visit interminable punishment on Evans and thereby make a lasting example of him. Small wonder that this pitiless virago hides behind a pseudonym and does not show her face. If I behaved as she did, I too would be unwilling to disclose my identity. The petition was a resounding success, attracting about 170,000 mouse-clicking subscribers: a depressing testimony both to its author's implacable malice and to human gullibility. Let no one pretend that honesty is always the best policy. It was their essential honesty in admitting to having intercourse with the girl that led to the prosecution of the two footballers and to Evans's conviction. It was Jean Hatchet's shameless and tendentious duplicity that did so much to prevent Evans's return to Sheffield. A fine lesson in morality, to be sure![27]

The facility with which people can subscribe to on-line petitions should in itself cause disquiet. An old school friend, who holds an

---

[27] The text of the on-line petition to the owners of Sheffield United FC is reproduced below. Note how this rambling rant sets up Evans as a symbolic scapegoat representing all men who have abused women, and therefore a proper object of severe and exemplary punishment.

Ched Evans was convicted of rape. It was a process of justice. To even consider reinstating him as a player at the same club is a deep insult to the woman who was raped and to all women like her who have suffered at the hands of a rapist. For the male leaders of the club to endorse him and "welcome him back" is an absolute humiliation to all women who expect the men who commit ***gross acts of violence*** *against women to pay for what they have done and part of that is relinquishing the celebrity they attained, and in this case used as a tool to facilitate the* ***violence****. The clear message to young boys and men is that you will be forgiven for this crime. Women will not be believed when they accuse you of that crime even if a court believes them. The message given is that men who commit such* ***atrocious crimes*** *will suffer only a small penance whilst the women they* ***attack*** *suffer for the rest of their lives. Sheffield United Football Club must not reinforce that message.*

Oxbridge doctorate and is certainly no fool, admitted to mouse-clicking this one, despite knowing nothing whatsoever of the details of the case. Once apprised of all the pertinent facts, he admitted that Evans was almost certainly the victim of a gross miscarriage of justice. I ask myself: How many of the subscribers to this petition and how many others who have railed against Evans share my friend's abysmal ignorance, and would, if they were better informed, renounce their hostility and adopt a more benign attitude? Ched Evans is certainly a victim of ignorance, much of it wilful.

4. Envy and Sanctimony

On 11 November 2014, three and a half weeks after his release from prison, Sheffield United FC announced that it would allow Evans to resume training with the club, while maintaining that no decision about his reinstatement as a player had yet been made. Later in the day it stated that its decision to permit him to train was in response to a request from the Professional Footballers' Association. This hiding behind the PFA was the first clear sign of the club's timidity. The Sheffield newspapers (*Star* and *Telegraph*) had already taken a hostile editorial stance against Evans and refused even to look at a short piece that I had written in his defence. Before long, they were joined by a handful of local politicians as well as minor celebrities, who counted themselves Sheffield United's patrons but now ostentatiously defected from this role.

One of the two local MPs who stuck his oar in was Nick Clegg, leader of the Liberal Democrats. One might have expected that, as such, he would have been keen to defend the time-honoured principle that ex-prisoners should be fully rehabilitated into society and, wherever possible, restored to their former occupation. Alas, any such hopes were doomed to disappointment. At a time when the electoral prospects of his party had never been so bleak,[28] he had no stomach to antagonise the screaming

---

[28] The Lib-Dems sustained devastating losses in the General Election on 7 May 2015. Their representation in Parliament was reduced from 57 to 8

sisterhood of radical feminists. And so, a noble principle was duly sacrificed to a mean expediency.

Add envy to the mixture that had been a-brewing and the concoction was indeed highly toxic. Bernard Mandeville defined envy as 'that baseness in our nature, which makes us grieve and pine at what we conceive to be a happiness in others'.[29] There are many features of Ched Evans's life which might expose him to this green-eyed monster. He is a good-looking young man with a loyal and forgiving girlfriend and a potential father-in-law whose supportiveness knows no bounds. Furthermore, he is endowed with a prodigious talent, which when deployed makes him an object of adulation and earns him a salary that few dare dream of. Mandeville – one of the most perceptive observers of human nature who ever lived – also pointed out that envy is something that no one is willing to acknowledge in himself. Therefore it cannot be indulged openly. In this case, however, it could be given free rein under the pretext of defending virtue and decency. Seldom can the stench of sanctimonious cant have hung so heavy over a town as it did over Sheffield at the end of 2014.

5. Betrayal

Towards the end of that week, the Olympic athlete Jessica Ennis-Hill declared that if Evans was allowed to resume his career with the club, she would insist that her name be removed from the stand which had been named in her honour. One club supporter, writing on a fans' website, pertinently questioned the motives of such people. Do they *really* see themselves as patrons and supporters of the club? Or do they merely pose as such for their own aggrandisement? Either way, they are superfluous appendages: small tails that should not be allowed under any circumstances to wag the much bigger dog. But wag the dog she did. Within less than a week SUFC had made an abject capitulation to the hostile

---

seats. Clegg retained his Sheffield seat, but with a greatly reduced majority, and resigned as Party Leader before noon the following day.

[29] *Fable of the Bees*, Remark N in the 1723 and subsequent editions. (*Fable*, Vol. 1, p.134).

forces, despite there being no evidence that the clamour raised against Evans was truly representative of either the club's supporters or the public at large.

On 20 November it withdrew the offer of allowing him to train and reneged on its long-standing and oft-repeated commitment to reinstate him to the team of which he had once been such a proud and highly respected member. Once again he became a victim: this time of abandonment and betrayal. On 21 November SUFC's co-chairman, Jim Phipps, made a pathetically feeble attempt to lay the blame for what had happened on the forces hostile to Evans. He ought rather to have acknowledged that his club's abandonment of Evans was an act of supine moral cowardice for which it alone was responsible. The wider ramifications of this caving in to pressure are considerable, reinforcing the message that duplicity and intimidation can easily triumph over intellectual and moral weakness.

6. Oldham: a Five Day Fiasco

The New Year of 2015 got off to a promising start. On 4 January the *Sunday Times* announced that a deal to sign Evans to a First Division club was imminent. By lunchtime, the BBC was reporting that a deal with Oldham Athletic was likely to be announced the next day. By Monday lunchtime the deal seemed to be in doubt and no announcement was made until 4.30 in the afternoon; and then it was only that there was to be no substantive statement. Negotiations were in progress during the next three days and a favourable outcome was predicted. However, by Thursday the deal had collapsed – ostensibly through fear of the withdrawal of financial sponsorship and acts of intimidation directed against the club's board members and staff. Once again the sinister forces of ochlocracy and demagogy[30] had triumphed.

Within minutes of the revelation that Oldham were going to sign Evans, the feminist cyber-bullies – no doubt fortified and encouraged by the easy victory they had enjoyed in Sheffield – had

---

[30] ochlocracy = mob rule; demagogy = rabble-rousing oratory.

launched a new petition, similar to the one addressed to SUFC. By this time, Evans had become so thoroughly demonized that all and sundry thought they could vilify him with little risk of recrimination.[31] Local and national politicians – ever on the lookout for opportunities to ingratiate themselves with shallow, capricious people – quickly weighed in against him, declaiming against the possibility of the projected signing. They were joined by the local diocesan bishop, Rt. Rev. David Walker, and the Police and Crime Commissioner and ex-Labour MP, Tony Lloyd. Both wantonly propagated the entirely false but virtually unchallenged notion that Evans was obdurately unrepentant and therefore a very unfit role model who should be disqualified from working as a professional footballer. If only they had had the sense to take to heart those six wise words of the Chinese leader Chairman Mao Tse-tung: 'No investigation, no right to speak!'[32]

At an early stage in my own examination of the facts and with very little expense of time or effort, I had seen the video that Evans had put on his website within days of his release from prison. He expressed unequivocally his regrets for the events which had led to his conviction, while maintaining his innocence of the crime of rape. To say that he was unrepentant was therefore a scurrilous calumny, but one that was industriously propagated by those who have no compunction about ignoring the truth if it threatens their personal interests or challenges the fashionable orthodoxies of political correctness.

7. Lessons and Role Models

Many of the scribblers and chatterers who took up their pens and wagged their tongues speculated on the message that would have been sent out by Ched Evans's prompt reinstatement to professional football. In my view, this message would have been a very salutary one: that a young man, who acknowledged that he had acted badly and had been punished for a crime which, with

---

[31] See Note 3. p. 30 below.

[32] *Quotations from Chairman Mao*, p.230. The theme of this paragraph is further explored in the next chapter.

good reason, he believes he did not commit, was being given a fresh chance. As things now stand, there is very little from which decent people can take comfort. The Crown Prosecution Service and the criminal justice system have once again been exposed to critical scrutiny and entirely warrantable cynicism.

Ignorance, duplicity, hypocrisy and sanctimonious claptrap were allowed to triumph over better informed and more benign forces. Sheffield United FC, which should have been among the most resolute of his supporters, will be seen by many as not only spineless and contemptible but utterly dishonoured and discredited. Throughout all that had happened, Evans himself was conspicuously reticent. He maintained a quiet dignity which puts to shame his detractors, be they of the strident or the mealy-mouthed variety. Now that he has been given the chance, Ched Evans may yet prove to be a better role model than they. As a victim of so much that is loathsome in human nature, he will at least continue to have my sympathy and support. There are many lessons to be learned from this sorry saga, and few of them are salutary. If you seek *bad* role models you need look no further than those who have taken the contrary part: to the duplicity and vindictiveness of 'Jean Hatchet'; to the opportunism of politicians and media pundits who jumped on the bandwagon that she set rolling; and to the owners of Sheffield United, who did not have the courage to stand by their principles and honour their promises.

Note 1. The Influence of Catherine MacKinnon

The following note is an extract from a letter of October 2008 from me to the American actor Alec Baldwin in response to his book ***A Promise to Ourselves*** *– an account of the bitter dispute between him and his ex-wife, Kim Basinger for access to their daughter. I had been in intermittent communication with him, as between 2002 and 2005 I had written an unpublished account of his life and work, one chapter of which treated the acrimonious breakdown of his marriage and the dispute over custody of his daughter. American spelling is retained. Passages in square brackets* […] *have been added.*

Chapter 14 [of your book] includes a transcription of a conversation you had at Harvard with Jeannie Suk, in the course of which she mentions Catherine MacKinnon (b. 1946) and her pervasive influence on how the US legal system views relations between the sexes (p.194). For reasons I shall make fully apparent, MacKinnon's writings are not something that I should ever bother to study in depth; however I have looked at the entry on her in *Sex from Plato to Paglia – a Philosophical Encyclopedia.* (It is the first entry in Vol. 2, immediately before my entry on Bernard Mandeville.) [Between 2002 and 2006 I served on the Advisory Board of this project and contributed five entries.]

Central to MacKinnon's output is her insistence that relationships between the two sexes are *characteristically* abusive and violent – a view she shared with her fellow radical feminist, Andrea Dworkin (1946-2005). MacKinnon goes so far as virtually to collapse the distinction between rape and consensual intercourse, since, she maintains, all relationships between men and women are essentially and necessarily flawed by the subordination on which they are based. This is not a scientific induction founded on wide empirical research but a dogma rooted in prejudice and maintained largely on *a priori*[33] grounds. The view to which it gives rise is surely – to say the least – grossly distorted. Like most people, in the course of my life I have seen among my family, friends and neighbors many instances of marriage or heterosexual cohabitation in which *both* participants seem to be quite happy. MacKinnon's disciples must renounce these everyday perceptions as delusional and erroneous. No amount of happy, smiling brides or contented housewives would be sufficient to support common sense beliefs.

It is not just that MacKinnon flies in the face of common sense: her doctrine is inconsistent with evolutionary theory. In all animals, a function as vital as reproduction must be prompted by instincts whose gratification – generally speaking at least – is pleasurable. This is exactly what we find. If women did not find

---

[33] *a priori* – a Latin phrase used in philosophy to characterise knowledge thought to be available without experience.

sexual relations with men satisfying, then they would constitute a very striking instance of mal-adaptation between an organism and its function, and human beings would not breed as prolifically as they do. MacKinnon would also have difficulty in explaining how, in our brave new world, women often make the running in sexual encounters and sometimes offer their favors with shameless abandon to men they hardly know. [The events which led to the trial of Ched Evans and Clayton McDonald constitute just such an instance.]

Writing this has reminded me of a joke I heard as a schoolboy forty-odd years ago [*i.e.* about 1964]:

- Why do rabbits have more fun than we do?
- Because there are more of them.
- Why are there more of them?
- Because they have more fun than we do.

This is facetious; and yet it embodies the important truth that sexual activity is enjoyable: whereas MacKinnon's doctrine, with all its pretentious gravity, rests on a lie.

I do not dispute the legitimacy of her concern for the welfare of women, but a dogma as palpably false as hers should be dismissed with ridicule and contempt or even castigated for its offensiveness. The true interests of women and of society as a whole are ill-served by such a blanket vilification of men. I therefore note with some alarm that she has enjoyed a lucrative and successful career and wields much influence. If such perverse ways of thinking have come not just to flourish in the ivory towers of academia but even to dominate state legislatures, then this is yet another reason why you had such a hard and painful ride in the courts of California; for the atmosphere must be poisoned by the presumption that men are guilty of violence and abuse. [There may well be reason to fear that 'such perverse ways of thinking' have now come to influence the prosecuting authorities in the UK.]

Note 2. The Perversity of the Disparate Verdicts

The jury may well have been influenced in its deliberations by the different circumstances in which McDonald and Evans came to be in the hotel room. The girl had determinedly attached herself to McDonald and travelled with him by taxi to the hotel. This surely indicated her consent to what was likely to follow – a consent which was not necessarily extended to, nor necessarily withheld from, Evans, who arrived later in response to a text message from McDonald. However, none of these factors renders Evans's conviction safe or even goes any way to supporting it; for – in all probability – he was convicted on the grounds that the girl lacked the *capacity* to consent by way of her inebriation. The jury did not specifically state this; but this was both the Prosecution's case and the surmise of the presiding judge – an opinion which it was perhaps unwise of him to make public in his sentencing remarks, as it paved the way firmly towards the contention that the disparity in the verdicts embodies an inconsistency. Some suspect that the judge was extremely surprised – and therefore unprepared – when the jury returned the two different verdicts.

Common sense and everyday experience dictate that if she had been too drunk to consent to copulate with Evans, she must almost certainly have been too drunk to consent to copulate with McDonald only a few minutes earlier. Consent cannot be given prospectively; so any consent suggested by the fact that the girl had voluntarily travelled to the hotel with McDonald would have been annulled by any subsequent incapacity and could not therefore be cited as justification for the disparity in the verdicts.

Six months after Evans's conviction, a court refused leave to appeal, declaring that there was *no* inconsistency in the disparate verdicts. Strictly speaking, this is true. It is *logically* possible that the girl's state of intoxication changed very rapidly, even though she consumed no more alcohol at the time in question. However, this is so highly improbable that without the strongest supporting evidence, no reasonable person would believe it, and no *responsible* jury would have convicted. There was no such evidence, and so, the disparity in the verdicts must be regarded as perverse. Judicial refusal to acknowledge this indicates that in 2012 the Court of Appeal was more concerned that the formalities of process had been duly followed than that justice had been done. This should surely excite alarm and evoke disgust in right-thinking people. The case highlights the dangers of bringing to trial cases where the evidence is tenuous to the point of vacuity. For what was at issue was not events in the physical world (sexual acts), nor the state of mind that authorised them (consent), but the *capacity* of one of the agents to give that consent. Had her incapacity been due to a permanent and readily verifiable condition such as imbecility, there would be no problem. Here, however, the alleged incapacity was ephemeral and impossible to gauge with the accuracy and certainty required to support a safe conviction.

On Wednesday 20 February 2013 at Southwark Crown Court, Mr Justice Sweeney, the presiding judge in the trial of Vicky Pryce,[34] refused to define the term *reasonable doubt*, but said that jurors must be 'sure'. I shall not comment on this judge's refusal to proffer a definition, apart from to say that his evasion might have been a wise one. Although the phrase exists in ordinary language, the concept it denotes is far from straightforward. It has exercised the minds of philosophers since ancient times and voluminous discussions about the nature of belief, doubt and knowledge have continued to pervade philosophical literature. It occurred to me that it might be useful to devise for the guidance of jurors a scale of probability, ranging from impossibility at zero to absolute certainty at 100. Such quantification of probability is common in games of chance and in areas which involve large quantities of data, such as actuarial tables and health statistics. It might be objected that such a scale of probability as I propose is

---

[34] The embittered ex-wife of the Liberal-Democrat politician Chris Huhn. After a second trial both she and her ex-husband were convicted of perverting the course of justice and sentenced to a period of imprisonment.

inappropriate, since legal cases generally involve issues that are not numerically quantifiable. Such a numerical model could, however, be defended if it served to render the matter more intelligible and thereby helped jurors to discharge their duty competently. The law requires that to secure conviction the prosecution must prove overwhelmingly the probability of guilt. There must be no room for reasonable doubt. I put it to a friend of judicial rank that in any trial the prosecution's case should attain a score well into the 90s if a conviction is to be deemed safe. He thought my suggestion eminently reasonable. In the case of Ched Evans, to suggest that his guilt was established by such a criterion would be preposterous – all the more so if his guilt was conjoined with the concession that his co-defendant was not guilty.

Note 3. The Nature of the Tabloid Press

One factor determining Ched Evans's treatment by tabloid journalists and feeding the animosity directed against him may be that just as newspapers have an interest in *reporting* bad news, so also have they an interest in *creating* it. His demonization ensured that his story could continue to be exploited. Bernard Mandeville's final work, the substantial pamphlet *A Letter to Dion* (1732) includes the following highly pertinent observation.

"The News-Writers, whose chief Business it is to fill their Papers and raise the Attention of their Readers, never forget any Scandal which can be publish'd with Impunity. By this Means a [Person] which once this Indignity has been put upon, is in a few Days render'd odious, and in less than a Fortnight comes to be infamous throughout the Kingdom, without any other Demerit. Those Polemick Authors among them...have a greater Regard to what will serve their Purpose, than they have to Truth or Sincerity. As they subsist by vulgar Errors, and are kept alive by the Spirit of Strife and Contention, so it is not their Business to rectify Mistakes in Opinion, but rather to encrease them when it serves their Turn." (pp. 8-9)

How little things have changed in almost three hundred years! There are honourable exceptions who have stood up for Evans's right to return to football. I mention David Walsh, Rod Liddell, Martin Samuel, Allison Pearson and Sarah Baxter.

4. Soundbite Thinking and Tabloid Moralizing

In the section dealing with the aborted attempt to sign Evans for Oldham Athletic, I named two individuals, who intervened – in my view malignly – as representatives of Church and State. These were Tony Lloyd, the Greater Manchester Police and Crime Commissioner and Rt. Rev. David Walker, the diocesan bishop. I have a letter from a spokesman for the former, which claims that "A central part of Tony's role is to be a voice for victims" and gives the text of his statement, which I reproduce below:

"Oldham Athletic Football Club should not sign Ched Evans. Ched Evans is a convicted rapist, and, while I strongly believe in the principle of rehabilitation, it will send out entirely the wrong message if they offer him a contract.

"All offenders have the right to rebuild their lives and make amends after they have served their sentence, but Ched Evans' lack of remorse and failure to acknowledge his offence means it is simply inappropriate for him to be on a Greater Manchester football pitch week in and week out presenting himself as some kind of role model, especially to young people."

I have ascertained that in the week of the Oldham fiasco the Bishop issued a tweet indicating that he had just done a piece for the TV programme *Granada Reports*: "Suggested that we remember the woman he raped + Unrepentant rapist can't be role model." *Twitter* – with its laconic restriction to 140 characters – would not be my medium of choice for communicating my thoughts on so complex and sensitive a subject. No Matter. Both these men made the same two main points: (1) that we have a duty to consider either one particular 'victim' or victims in general; and (2) that Evans was unrepentant. Their statements are far too glib to do the subject justice. As I have already established, and demonstrate again in the letters reproduced below, the claim that Evans had shown no remorse is palpably false. While he steadfastly maintained that he was no rapist, he none the less acknowledge that he had indeed acted badly and expressed regret for this.[35] The 'Thesis of Unrepentance' is either a malicious or a wanton fabrication, largely created and sustained by hostile media but easily exposed for the monstrosity it is. For people such as Tony Lloyd and the Bishop to have endorsed it is scandalous. I shall be charitable enough to suppose that they did not make this false claim *knowing* it to be untrue. Even so, their obvious failure to make adequate enquiries is in itself gravely reprehensible.[36]

The other point – that we have a duty to victims – might *seem* fair and reasonable; but what does it actually *mean*? What, if any, are the practical implications of these words in this context? As I have argued at length, the particular 'victim' in this case was a victim of the folly and opportunism of the Crown Prosecution Service in bringing the case to trial, but not of Ched Evans. But even if Evans had been guilty and she did indeed have a genuine claim to victimhood at his hands, what more could she expect? Even genuine victims are not entitled to have their aggressors subjected to interminable or disproportionate punishment, nor to deprive them of the chance to earn a living. Evans had already been quite severely punished in accordance with the law. Neither she nor the vociferous partisans of the anti-Ched Evans bandwagon had any right to exact any more from him. Their cause is an entirely illegitimate one, quite inconsistent with the rule of law, and should be denounced as such. In no way should it have been pandered to by politicians, high-ranking officials or prominent churchmen, who were – perhaps unscrupulously – capitalizing on the misfortunes of all parties in an endeavour to ingratiate themselves by saying what they imagined people want to hear.

---

[35] The credibility of his expressions of regret is corroborated by the fact that they were accepted by persons very close to him, who would have most to lose from his bad faith. His partner, Natasha and her father Karl Massey would not have supported him so staunchly had they doubted his sincerity. Nor, for that matter, would I. Of course, the virulent rancour that was raised against Evans was such that *no* manifestation of contrition would ever have been sufficient to placate it.

[36] See Endnote (p.41) – The Ethics of Belief.

Yet this is precisely what happened, even to the extent that significant attempts were made to legitimize this agenda. Ed Miliband, who in the week of the Oldham fiasco was attending a conference in Manchester, said that he would not like to be in their shoes if Oldham Athletic signed Evans. His shadow Sports Minister, Clive Efford, approached the Football Association and urged that, if the signing went ahead, they should refuse to license Evans, thus preventing him from working.

The FA has the very proper role of punishing offences *within and against the game*: for example, match-fixing, aggression by players against one another; intimidation or assaults on referees. However, they would be very foolish indeed to pick up the poisoned chalice proffered by Clive Efford and extend their remit to inflicting additional penalties on players for offences, acknowledged or disputed, that had already been punished within the criminal justice system. To have acted against Evans in the way proposed would have put the FA in a particularly invidious position. It would have entailed blighting for ever the career of a young man whose record on the pitch was unblemished, for a conviction which – even if not overturned – would always have been disputed, and which had been imposed as a result of an indiscretion committed at the age of only 22. To echo Miliband's words: I should not want to be in their shoes if they were seen to act thus.

If Miliband and his henchman (or their successors) want Ched Evans and others in comparable situations to be debarred from working, they should seek to introduce legislation to this effect. I do not wish them success, and I am certain they will enjoy none. This primrose path to an illusory populism might seem enticing, but it would quickly lead to a moral, political, and legal quagmire. Would the legislation be confined to sportsmen and women? Or would it extend to others with a prominent public *persona* – perhaps to actors and musicians? Would it specify that a man who had broken some law could not have a leading role in a TV soap but might be employed in a small local theatre? That he could not be a solo violinist or the leader of an orchestra but might be allowed to play second fiddle on the back benches?

Under their tentative proposal, would Luke McCormack have been allowed to return to Plymouth Argyle after killing two children by drunken driving? For many years the actor Leslie Grantham enjoyed a leading role in the BBC TV soap opera *EastEnders*, though he had spent ten years in prison for murdering a taxi driver while serving as a soldier in West Germany in 1966. Was it ever suggested that his employment as a television actor 'sent out the wrong message' or incited viewers to become murderers? I very much doubt it.

There are no clear lines of demarcation either in offences or in proscribed occupations and it would be impracticable to impose any. On 7 January, 2015 Clive Efford said: "The decision on whether players should return to football after committing serious offences is not a matter solely for individual clubs and I have asked the FA to refuse his [Evans's] registration…" I disagree. Such decisions should indeed be left in the hands of those that are most affected by them. I am firmly of the view that the owners and management of both Sheffield United and Oldham Athletic believed in Ched Evans's essential innocence. In any case, they wanted to give him a second chance. It is profoundly regrettable that so many hostile forces conspired to prevent this. The time may well be nigh when both the FA and the PFA will need to take a more forthright stand to defend the principles which I have enunciated above. The sooner they do so, the better.

Letter to Tony Lloyd, Greater Manchester Police & Crime Commissioner

16 January 2015

Dear Mr Lloyd,

Thank you for the response from [one of your administrators] to my letter of 6 January, claiming that your statement (the text of which was appended to your letter) was 'clear, balanced and reasonable'. Your statement might indeed impress the shallow people at whom it is aimed; but neither it nor your subsequent attempt at self-justification cuts any ice with me.

Your main problem – to my mind an insuperable one – is that your remarks rest on the grotesquely false assumption that Ched Evans has shown no remorse. This is demonstrably untrue. Within days of his release he expressed regret for the sordid events which led to his conviction, while continuing to maintain his innocence of the crime of rape. He was constrained by the Probation Service to remove this video from his website, but it is still readily accessible on the internet.

In the three months since leaving prison Mr Evans's conduct has been entirely unexceptionable. Some might even think it exemplary. Having endured a period of incarceration for a crime he probably did not commit, he was confronted on his release by a multitude of enemies, many of whom, like yourself, are abysmally ill-informed – perhaps wilfully so. Despite repeated assurances of reinstatement to the team, his former club, Sheffield United, abandoned him. In such a situation. I should feel bitter and resentful, and certainly not in a frame of mind to make any concessions to those who wish me nothing but ill.

In fairness to you, I admit that other public figures (including the Bishop of Manchester, Rt. Rev. David Walker) have gone down the same reckless path as you. Before making any pronouncements, a public figure should take every care to ascertain all the relevant facts. I believe the current jargon is '***due diligence***'. Such a duty is particularly incumbent on those who are bent on maligning another's reputation in so grave a matter as this.

All that has taken place is being duly noted, and will one day be put on permanent record in a book. If no one else wants to do it, I will. The enclosed short book [*The Prosecutor Unmask'd*] explains why I have so little confidence in the probity of people in high places, one of whom [Sir Kier Starmer] is now a parliamentary candidate for your party.[37]

Yours sincerely,

J. Martin Stafford

---

[37] Sir Kier Starmer was elected to Parliament as the Labour MP for Holborn & St Pancras (London) in the General Election of 7 May, 2015.

Letter in *Oldham Evening Chronicle*,

Friday 16 January 2015

I was very sorry to learn of the collapse of the deal to sign Ched Evans to OAFC. Having seen the media coverage of the affair, two things particularly concern me. The first is the widespread misapprehension that he is unrepentant. Within days of his release from prison, Ched Evans posted on his website a short video expressing his profound regret for the events of the night which led to his conviction, while continuing to maintain his innocence of the crime of rape. I am informed that he was forced by the Probation Service to remove this from his website, though it is still accessible on You-tube.

The second is the intervention of Tony Lloyd, the local Police and Crime Commissioner, who has propagated the aforementioned error by speaking of Mr Evans's 'lack of remorse' and expressed his opposition to Evans's rehabilitation to the game. Whatever Tony Lloyd's private opinion, his public and official stance on this subject should have been one of impartial detachment. Neither OAFC, by seeking to sign Evans, nor Evans himself, by trying to regain employment in his profession, was acting amiss. Tony Lloyd's intervention is therefore both ill-informed and grossly improper. I hope that Latics supporters and other local people who share my sense of grievance will address their complaints to: Donna Hall, Lead Chief Officer, Greater Manchester Police and Crime Panel, c/o Jeanette Staley, Rochdale Borough Council, Floor 3, Number One Riverside, Smith Street, Rochdale, OL16 1XU, or by email to: jeanette.staley@rochdale.gov.uk

As I no longer live in Greater Manchester, I lack the status to complain. I am, however, encouraging Manchester people that I know to take action.

J. Martin Stafford, SOLIHULL

Letter to the Rt. Rev. David Walker, Bishop of Manchester

23 January 2015

Dear David,

I am pleased to say that since our recent email correspondence, on Friday 16 January the *Oldham Evening Chronicle* published a letter in which I deplore the intervention of Tony Lloyd, your local Police and Crime Commissioner, and his characterisation of Ched Evans as unrepentant. In a letter to him (copy enclosed) I pointed out that this calumny against Ched Evans is one that you too seem to have committed. While I am reluctant to impute bad motives to you, I think you have been ill-advised and much less cautious than you might have been. Your own positon is not quite like that of Tony Lloyd, who (in my view) has a duty of complete impartiality that you may not share. Also, while I have seen his written statement, I have seen only reports of your own intervention (made on the radio) and your remarks in our private email exchange.

Neither of you seems to have taken into account the video that Ched Evans made shortly after leaving prison in which he clearly acknowledged that he acted wrongly. This surely amounts to remorse. My own view is that he was hardly any more at fault than his co-defendant or the girl who was a party to those sordid proceedings – the so-called 'victim'. Since he has acknowledged his wrongdoing and served time in prison, he ought, like others in his situation, to be able to resume his career without further delay. The *Oldham Evening Chronicle* of 9 January published a selection of Facebook and Twitter comments, one of which expressed surprise that you are not on his side. The same thought had crossed my own mind.

I have now added to my document, *A Catalogue of Woes*, a new section briefly adumbrating the events in Oldham in which I mention you by name, and a long endnote[38] explaining why the verdict of *guilty* must be regarded as highly contentious. The conviction for rape was on a legal technicality of fairly recent invention and even on that basis was very unsafe. I wrote this new note to take account of comments in a blog that you brought to my attention. For this I am grateful, as it prompted me to address this crucial aspect of the case once again, to clarify the issues in my own mind, and to render my argument as watertight as possible. All this material will be published when Ched's appeal process is complete: if not by someone else, then under the *Ismeron* imprint of which I have exclusive control.

A passage in Dugald Stewart (1753-1828)[39] prompted me to read the sermon 'On the Government of the Tongue' – one of fifteen delivered by Joseph Butler (1692-1752) at the Rolls Chapel in 1726. Towards the end of it,[40] Butler (later to become Bishop of Bristol and then of Durham) makes the point – and to my mind it is no less pertinent and salutary now than it was then – that when we speak ill of others, the sins we lay to their charge must be real; and of this we must have the utmost assurance. For if they are not, we do them a grave injustice. That Ched Evans has been convicted is certainly true; that he really is a rapist seems very doubtful indeed; that he has shown no repentance is manifestly false.

---

[38] Note 2, p.29 above.

[39] It was in Volume II of Stewart's last book, *The Philosophy of the Active and Moral Powers of Man* (published in the year of his death) that I came across the reference to Butler's Sermons. On the same page (279) is a passage commending the freedom of the press and suggesting that everyone should be allowed 'openly to avow his opinions, [but not] without the sanction of his name'. How he would have deplored the advent of social media and on-line petitions, with their guarantees of anonymity and the abrogation of personal responsibility that this entails. Stewart was Professor of Moral Philosophy at Edinburgh between 1785 and 1810. Though now neglected, in his lifetime he was much revered, and is commemorated by a monument on Calton Hill (Edinburgh) – one of the most handsome ever erected to a philosopher.

[40] *Sermons* p. 80.

Perhaps it is part of your role as a bishop in the established church never to challenge, but rather to acquiesce in, the criminal convictions delivered by our courts. You also seem to be more comfortable than I am with the idea of making scapegoats of people. This may be because one particular instance of scapegoating is so central to orthodox Christian theology.[41]

I have no doubt that in other jurisdictions or in in our own not so long ago Ched Evans would not have been put on trial. That he was is largely due to a change in policy – in my view opportunistic and tending to corrupt – on the part of the CPS. See my little book *The Prosecutor Unmask'd* (copy enclosed), which deals with the decision to prosecute Michael Le Vell for raping ________. For legal reasons she could not be identified….within its pages.[42] I believe that in putting this man on trial the last Director of Public Prosecutions, Kier Starmer, and his advisor, Alison Levitt, effectively conspired to pervert the course of justice – a crime which the offices they held allowed them to commit with complete impunity. You will understand why, in the light of such events, I am deeply sceptical of the probity of those elevated to such offices, many of whom may well be self-serving opportunists, hypocrites and downright liars.

You ask if there is anything else that you can do. I do not know. If Ched's conviction is upheld, will you then say it is time to draw a line under his offence and allow him to resume his career? Such a pronouncement would be constructive, though somewhat belated. If, as I hope, his conviction is overturned, then the tardy support of those who were once against him would probably serve little purpose and might even be unwelcome.

Yours sincerely,

Martin Stafford

---

[41] That by his death on the cross, Christ redeemed the sins of the world.

[42] For the same legal reasons, the identity of this malicious and discredited complainant cannot be published here either, but it does appear in the original letter from me to the Bishop.

Note. The Ethics of Belief.

A society is damaged by the dissemination of falsehood no less than an environment is polluted by smoking chimneys and toxic effluent. An eloquent antidote to the poison so irresponsibly infused by Tony Lloyd and David Walker in maintaining that Ched Evans was unrepentant is to be found in an essay by the secularist Victorian scholar and mathematician William Kingdon Clifford (1845-79). In the first part of 'The Ethics of Belief' (1877)[43] Clifford – in salutary contrast to the practice of these cavalier Mancunian meddlers – enjoins his readers always to make diligent enquiries and thereby ensure that their beliefs are adequately warranted by the evidence.

"The question of right or wrong has to do with the origin of [a man's] belief, not the matter of it; not what it was, but how he got it; not whether it turned out to be true or false, but whether he had a right to believe on such evidence as was before him" (178).

Of hypothetical people known to have made false allegations he says:

"...although they had sincerely and conscientiously believed in the charges they had made, yet *they had no right to believe on such evidence as was before them*. Their sincere convictions, instead of being honestly earned by patient inquiring, were stolen by listening to the voice of prejudice and passion (179)....And it might be said to [them], 'However convinced you were of the justice of your cause and the truth of your convictions, you ought not to have made a public attack upon any man's character until you had examined the evidence on both sides with the utmost patience and care.' (180)."

How very apposite Clifford's words seem in this case.

---

[43] *Lectures and Essays*, Vol II, 177-211. First published in the *Contemporary Review*, January, 1877.

5. Hanging Ched – Double Jeopardy in the Court of Public Opinion

Stuart Gilhooly

This essay was posted briefly on the Irish PFA website on 17 November 2014. It was removed in response to protests from feminist pressure groups.

It's hard to like Ched Evans. He cheats on his girlfriend. By having sex with a young girl who has just performed the same act with his mate while he watches. And other friends peer through the window. In the pantheon of tawdry escapades that young men with too much money engage in, it's as tacky as it is immoral. Having spent 2½ years in prison after being found guilty of rape, he then refuses to apologise and makes a ham-fisted, cringe-inducing video in which his loyal girlfriend is so embarrassed she can't look at the camera.

So far, so standard. Another hang-Ched-out-to-dry article. Never let him play football again. Anything else but not football. Because football is the moral guardian of our society. Are we all clear on that? No bad boys in football anymore or everyone resigns. Wait. I've an idea. It's radical but if you bear with me, you might agree. Let's take a closer look at the facts. Examine Ched's alleged crime and maybe make a merit-based decision on his life time punishment. Still with me? Good.

Ched Evans, Sheffield United and Wales striker, and his footballer friend, Clayton McDonald, went on a night out. On his way home alone, Clayton meets a girl. She had been drinking. She returns to his hotel with him, according to his uncontroverted evidence, at her request. CCTV shows both of them leaving a taxi. While she is clearly not sober, she is able to walk in high heels and lift a pizza box off the ground. In the meantime, McDonald has texted Evans to say he is with a girl and the clear implication is that Evans should join him. He duly does this and they both have sex with her. McDonald leaves by the front door and Evans by the fire exit, at different times. Both were present, however, while the other was having sex. Friends of theirs attempted to watch through the window.

She wakes the next morning and says she remembers nothing. She is missing her handbag (which she left outside a takeaway) and decides later to report this to the police. She claims not to recall any sex or even meeting McDonald. By tracing the players through the room booking and CCTV, both McDonald and Evans are interviewed and admit to having sex with her. There is no DNA evidence and there is no evidence of any force. After making the admissions of having sex with her, both have effectively ensured a criminal investigation. Prior to this, an allegation of rape wasn't even contemplated due to her lack of recall. Both men were tried and bizarrely, Evans was convicted while McDonald was acquitted.

Let's examine this for a minute. There are three people in the room. Two say the sex with both men was consensual and that she was not too drunk to consent. The other says she remembers absolutely nothing. The only other person with any small contribution to make as to what occurred in the room is the night porter who hears noises coming from the room of a sexual nature, the voices being both male and female. There is no suggestion of coercion or reluctance. The prosecution case is that she was too drunk to consent. Yet the jury acquit McDonald and convict Evans despite the fact that the two acts occur within a matter of minutes of one another. There is no evidence of her having had any drink between meeting McDonald and the two sexual acts.

Presumably, the jury thinking is that she met McDonald and offered to go back to his hotel so this was a form of consent. If so, it makes no sense. She says she doesn't recall meeting him and she had no more to drink after this. If anything, presumably the passage of time would have sobered her up rather than making her more intoxicated. Most importantly, there isn't a shred of independent evidence to suggest that she was too drunk to consent at the moment that she had sex with either man. Indeed, there is no evidence at all as even she doesn't know what state of intoxication she was in.

None of this should be taken to suggest that the girl in question has done anything wrong. She hasn't. The reality is that this is a scene that is played out in every town in England, and no doubt Ireland, every weekend. Anyone who believes that some young adults in their late teens or 20s are not engaging in sexual acts with multiple partners is either incredibly naïve or utterly deluded. Clearly, it is a minority pursuit but it happens and it happens regularly. Many of these participants are drunk. The degree of intoxication no doubt varies but it leads us to the key question: what is too drunk to consent? How does a man determine whether or not a potential partner falls into this category? The facetious answer might be a test to walk in a straight line or even a breathalyser. Of course, these are not realistic but it helps to consider the criteria when dealing with this very sensitive and nuanced legal point.

Is it a subjective test? In other words, if she says I don't remember anything, is that enough? Clearly that can't be right, so where does this begin and end? There is little point in trying to dissect the legal niceties of this very complex issue but suffice to say that Ched Evans has a very arguable case that he is the victim of a miscarriage of justice. **If having sex with a drunk woman is rape then thousands of men are guilty of rape every day.** The simple point is that degrees of intoxication are a very difficult concept for young men to grapple with when they themselves have had plenty to drink.

So, let's get to the point, should Ched Evans be allowed back in football? Clearly, if he has been a victim of miscarriage of justice then he should. However, let's just say, for the sake of argument, that he is guilty and knew he was having sex with a woman that was too drunk to consent. In those circumstances, he has deservedly received a five year sentence and the consequences that flow from a conviction for a sexual offence. Rape is a horrific crime which, upon rightful conviction, should always be punished by a custodial sentence.

The difficult element of this discussion, though, is the part about the scale of the crime. There are people who will say rape is rape and degrees shouldn't come into it but in sentencing these issues matter. This crime, as alleged, was at the bottom end. There was no violence and thankfully the victim has no recollection of it. This, I hasten to add, does not make it right, or anything close to it, but it is nonetheless a mitigating factor. Ched Evans served half of his sentence and will be a registered sex offender for the rest of his life. He has most likely missed out on the best part of his career and will forever be vilified for the alleged crime. Football is a popular pastime but the idea that all of its participants should be candidates for beatification[44] is ridiculous.

We all recall the public opprobrium that greeted the return to football of convicted felons, Lee Hughes and Luke McCormick? Don't we? Maybe not. For those who didn't hear the muted, almost silent response to the rehabilitation of these two killers into football, here's a reminder. Both Hughes and McCormick were found guilty of dangerous driving causing death. In the case of McCormick, he was drunk and killed two children.

When they had served their sentences, they both returned to football at Football League clubs. McCormick is currently captain of Plymouth Argyle. Hughes played league football until the age of 37 and is still playing in the Conference. While there may have

---

[44] [beatification = the act by which the Catholic Church declares that a deceased person may be venerated. This is sometimes followed by canonization – the declaration that he or she is a saint. See entries in *The Oxford Dictionary of the Christian Church*, pages 145 and 230. JMS]

been some discussion about the return of these players to football, I can recall no serious suggestion that they should not be signed by any club. Which is as it should be. They, like Evans, have served their time. Their crimes, which seem undisputed unlike Evans, were arguably worse but either way, they deserve a second chance at life.

Perhaps the difference between them and Evans is that they showed remorse and apologised for their actions. But how can Evans apologise? He is convinced, and has a good argument, that he is not guilty of rape. If he apologised, then he is admitting a crime he feels he didn't commit. Who would do that? There are certain jobs to which you cannot return as a convicted felon but there is always a reason. The argument that a League One footballer is a role model and therefore his career must end is particularly specious.

Would this happen in the League of Ireland? **Leaving aside the conclusion that a set of facts similar to the Evans case would never see the light of day in an Irish courtroom, it's hard to see how the sanctimony which has pervaded the discussion in the English media would be tolerated in this jurisdiction.** From Jessica Ennis-Hill to Charlie Webster and pretty much every media commentator who has waded into this mire, the horses most of these pundits have mounted are so high, they'll need a parachute to get down. When sanctimony takes over, there is rarely any real room for serious debate.

It now appears that Sheffield United have been swayed by the verdict of the court of public opinion. Ched Evans is toxic, don't touch him with a bargepole. From a media and marketing point of view, that's probably right. And money always talks. But Ched Evans has served his time, whether he is innocent or guilty. He puts the ball in the net so eventually someone will take a chance on him.

In the meantime, however, he continues to serve his sentence. Those who know little about his case will continue to vilify him while ignoring the fact that if it was their son, brother, friend or relative in the same position, they would fight tooth and nail to defend his name. It's not easy to muster up too much sympathy for Evans but there is surely nothing worse than being accused of a crime which you genuinely believe you didn't commit.[45] The argument against that is that a jury convicted him of the crime. That's right. And the same applied to the Guildford Four and the Birmingham Six. They got no public sympathy either. Maybe he is guilty or perhaps he's innocent, none of us knows for sure. Surely, either way, he deserves a chance at redemption. Don't we all?

Stuart Gilhooly is the solicitor to the Professional Football Association of Ireland. He is also a journalist and in 2014 was shortlisted, for the fifth year in succession, as Journalist of the Year at the Irish Magazine Awards. In January 2015 he was appointed to sit in the Court of Arbitration for Sport.

---

[45] [This same point is made very poignantly by Adam Smith in a passage added to the sixth edition of *The Theory of Moral Sentiments*, published in 1790 – the year of Smith's death: "Unmerited reproach is….frequently capable of mortifying very severely even men of more than ordinary constancy… An innocent man…is often not only shocked, but most severely mortified by the serious, though false, imputation of a crime; especially when that imputation happens unfortunately to be supported by some circumstances which give it an air of probability." (119) JMS]

6. Summary and Conclusions

Apart from the wantonness and folly of the three principal agents on that fateful night in the hotel room near Rhyl, a number of human agencies subsequently contributed to the manifold mischief and misery that ensued. In my view, all of these are to some degree intellectually discredited and certainly – by virtue of their status – almost as reprehensible as the original three miscreants.

§1. The opportunism of the Crown Prosecution Service. I have already discussed this on pages 16-7. If the tone of an organisation is determined by those who lead it, then given that the Director of Public Prosecutions at the time was Kier Starmer – elevated to knighthood in 2013 and elected as a Labour MP in May, 2015 – it is hardly surprising if a culture of unprincipled opportunism prevailed.[46]

§2.1 The jury, which returned the disparate verdicts. I wonder how any person of sound mind and even moderate intelligence, having due regard to the paucity of the evidence, could have acquitted one of the two co-defendants and convicted the other. There was not a shred of evidence to indicate that the girl had not consented. Though there *was* evidence that she had been drinking, it fell far short of proving that she was too inebriated to consent to sexual activity. And if she had been, then she must also have been too inebriated to consent to sexual activity with the other defendant only a few minutes earlier.

---

[46] See my short book *The Prosecutor Unmask'd* for an account of the unscrupulous way in which in February 2013 the CPS in London ordered the prosecution of the *Coronation Street* actor Michael Le Vell on the basis of allegations that they well knew were almost certainly both false and malicious. The chief prosecutor for the North West, Mr Nazir Afzal, (based in Manchester) had decisively dismissed the case 13½ months earlier. When I wrote that book in the spring of 2014, I was not aware of Starmer's ambitions to launch himself into a political career partly by posing as a champion of the victims of sexual abuse.

§2.2 It is possible that the jury felt that Evans's role in the events of that night was *morally* more reprehensible than that of McDonald and that this factor improperly influenced them. It is also possible that the timing of their deliberations (a Friday afternoon) spurred them to arrive at too hasty a verdict. Had they not reached a decision, some of them would have had to embark on a fourth week of jury service: an experience they might have been reluctant to undergo. By sparing themselves this trouble, they subjected Evans to an ordeal infinitely worse and helped to bring the criminal justice system into disrepute. I concede that one is bound to have *some* sympathy with jurors who have to deal with such cases. Their duty is certainly not a pleasant one.

§3. The first Court of Appeal sitting in November 2012, constrained as it was by a legalistic mindset. The disparity in the verdicts ought to have set metaphorical alarm bells ringing loudly in the heads of the appeal judges, just as it did in my own head. Notoriously, judges do not like to intervene in matters of fact. This is the domain of the jury; and so they deployed the most convoluted, casuistic and disingenuous of reasoning to justify the perverse outcome of the trial, and refused to allow the case to go to appeal. If the law incorporates the general principle that the benefit of any doubt should always favour the accused, on this occasion that principle was horribly violated.

§4. The duplicitous and vindictive on-line petition. It is difficult to know precisely how influential this was – possibly very. On pages 20-1, I have criticised its highly tendentious wording. It should have been rejected out of hand by anyone who had taken the trouble to look dispassionately at the facts of the case. However, it probably determined subsequent events by stifling temperate discussion and fostering a climate of near-hysteria.[47] The day after SUFC announced that it would not reinstate Evans to the team, the editor of *The Sheffield Star* expressed the view on

[47] hysteria = a frenzied state of mind that was once believed to arise from the womb. The word *hysteria*, like *hysterectomy*, is derived from the Greek word for womb.

the BBC Radio 4 *Today* programme that the intervention of Ennis-Hill was probably what finally tipped the balance against Evans.

§5. The weak leadership of SUFC. The decision of the club's owners to drop Ched Evans was both a considerable shock and a great disappointment to me. I firmly believed at the time that they had always intended to restore him to the team, as they had given every indication of this. I subsequently learned that this undertaking had been repeated on several occasions during the time of his imprisonment. As an honourable man, I believe that one is bound to discharge obligations that one has voluntarily contracted. The owners of SUFC are undoubtedly very wealthy men who could have resisted the pressures to which they were subjected and stood firmly by their resolution to do what was right. In my view, they were far too easily deflected from this path. They should not have been deflected from it at all.

§6. The Tabloid Press. It would be naïve in the extreme to expect the tabloid press to exert a benign influence in situations such as the Ched Evans affair. I cannot do better than to refer my readers again to the passage from Mandeville's *A Letter to Dion* (see page 31 above). He describes them to a tee.

§7.1 Politicians. At a time when sound and principled moral leadership was called for, politicians gave none. They either sat on the fence with mealy-mouthed equivocation (David Cameron[48] and Nick Clegg) or came out firmly against Evans's restoration to a career in football (Ed Miliband, Clive Efford and Tony Lloyd). Little wonder that in the course of an interview on a Dublin radio station, an Oldham Athletic board member, Barry Owen, declared that what had transpired made him feel ashamed to be British.[49] Mr Owen was disgusted by the fact that although Evans had suffered the *weight* of the law when he was convicted, he did not

---

[48] David Cameron's failure to support Evans after his release from prison was incongruous with remarks he made on 8 February 2016 to the effect that prisoners should be seen as 'potential assets' whose rehabilitation should be encouraged. Perhaps he experienced a change of heart.

[49] *Oldham Evening Chronicle*, 24 Feb 2015.

enjoy the full *protection* of the law in his legitimate quest for employment and full rehabilitation. His sentiments are ones that I share.

§7.2 By lunchtime on the day after the General Election (8 May 2015) Nick Clegg and Ed Miliband had resigned as leaders of their respective parties, both of which had fared very badly in the previous day's polls. I felt some sympathy for Nick Clegg, whom I regard as being a generally honourable man. In the aftermath of the 2010 General Election, he had gone into coalition with the Conservatives in order to effect a stable government and forestall another possibly devastating financial crisis. By doing this, he put country before party and subsequently paid a very high price, seeing his party's parliamentary representation almost wiped out in 2015. In the course of his dignified resignation speech as party leader, he berated the political forces that had played on fear and grievance rather than appealing to generosity. His words well characterise those who had demonised Ched Evans. Ironically, by his equivocation in October 2014, Nick Clegg had failed to come to Ched's support when he should have done; but his conduct was far less culpable than that of Ed Miliband, who – in a spirit of unscrupulous opportunism – had come out firmly against Evans during the Oldham fiasco.

7. Chronology of the Main Events

2011

May 30: 'The day after the night before'. Ched Evans is arrested on suspicion of sexual assault at the Premier Inn, Rhuddlan, near Rhyl, North Wales.

July 26 – *i.e.* eight weeks later: Ched Evans and fellow footballer Clayton McDonald are charged with rape.

2012

April 20: At Caernarvon Crown Court Evans is jailed for five years for rape but McDonald is acquitted. Evans maintains his innocence.

April 24: Evans's lawyers announce that he is to appeal against his conviction.

August 21: The first stage of Evans's appeal is rejected after a judge had refused his application for leave to appeal against his conviction.

November 6: Evans is again refused leave to appeal after his case is rejected by three judges at the Court of Appeal in London.

2014

April 18: After reports that Sheffield United intend to re-sign Evans, an online petition is launched urging them not to do so.

October 13: During this week I begin to take an interest in the case (of which I was previously unaware) after learning that broadcaster Judy Finnigan had suffered abuse merely for questioning the objectives of the anti-Ched Evans campaign.

October 17: Evans is released from prison after serving half of his five year sentence and a statement is released on his website saying that he will continue to fight to clear his name.

October 18: SUFC release a statement to the effect that they are 'continuing to deliberate on any long-term decision' after media reports emerge that they have offered Evans a contract.

October 19: The Criminal Cases Review Commission confirms that it is to fast-track Evans's case to investigate whether his conviction should be referred to the Court of Appeal.

October 22: Evans releases a statement affirming his desire to return to football and says: 'Even though I have been released from prison, I am determined to continue the fight to clear my name and it is public knowledge that an application to refer my case back to the Court of Appeal has recently been submitted to the Criminal Cases Review Commission by my lawyers.'

October 31: I phone the *Sheffield Star* and offer them a short piece I had written entitled 'Why I support Ched Evans'. They refuse even to look at it.

November 6: I have lunch with Karl Massey and pledge to do whatever I can to help Ched.

November 11: SUFC confirm that Evans will return immediately to train with the club following a request from the Professional Footballers' Association, but state that they are 'not prepared at this time' to make a decision on whether to re-sign him.

November 12: Sheffield Central MP Paul Blomfield urges SUFC to change their decision. Deputy Prime Minister Nick Clegg says the club must 'think really long and hard' before deciding whether to allow Evans to play for them again.

November 13: Olympic Gold Medalist Jessica Ennis-Hill issues a statement announcing that she has told SUFC she would want her name removed from the Bramall Lane stand should Evans be offered a contract to play for the club.

November 17: Stuart Gilhooly's piece is posted for a very short time on the Irish PFA website. (By coincidence, the centenary of the birth of my father, Ernest Stafford.)

November 20: SUFC announce that they have retracted the offer for Evans even to train with the club and will not reinstate him to the team.

2015

January 4-8: The five days in which it seemed for a time that Oldham Athletic FC would recruit Evans.

September 15-6: After ***eleven months*** of investigation, a CCRC panel meets to discuss Evans's case and decides to undertake yet more investigations.

October 5: Acknowledging that information not disclosed at the trial might have affected the verdict, the CCRC refers the case to the Court of Appeal.

2016

March 2: It is announced that the Court of Appeal will convene to deal with the case on March 22.

March 22-3: After a hearing over two days, on which reporting restrictions are imposed, the three appeal judges defer their judgment until April.

April 21: Four years and a day after his conviction, it is now overturned and a retrial called for, as the court recognises that new evidence submitted at the appeal might well have affected the outcome of the original trial. Reporting restrictions are maintained on the nature of this new evidence.

May 27: A hearing at Cardiff Crown Court sets the date of the retrial for 4 October, the presiding judge to be Mrs Justice Nicola Davies.

June 20: Chesterfield FC Chairman, Dave Allen, announces that after careful consideration the club has offered Evans a one year contract. "Chesterfield FC have given a great deal of thought to this signing and following the court's decision, we are in no doubt that Ched Evans should be welcomed back into his profession as a professional footballer." The statement also made clear that the Team Manager, Danny Wilson, and the First Team Coach, Chris Morgan, know Ched from their days with him at Sheffield and that both regard him very highly.

July 4: Ched starts training with his new team.

July 23: In his debut match for Chesterfield FC (a friendly against Ilkeston) Ched scores his first goal.

October 4-14: After a trial lasting eight days, in the course of which there was presented significant new evidence discrediting the 'complainant', and undermining the prosecution's already feeble case, Evans was unanimously acquitted after less than three hours.

8. Postscript: The Confrontation with Reality

On 21 April 2016, the Court of Appeal overturned Evans's conviction, but, in compliance with the wishes of the Crown Prosecution Service, sent the case for retrial, ruling that in this unusual case evidence from two new witnesses relating to the complainant's sexual history should be presented. Only the jury knows how influential this new evidence was in securing Evans's acquittal. Predictably, its admission by the court precipitated alarm among people keen to facilitate complaints of, and secure convictions for, sexual offences. A door which had long been closed was now partially reopened. Perhaps this is a case which highlights the need for people to be careful about what they wish for. Had Ched Evans not been so irresponsibly prosecuted, or if his conviction had been overturned at a much earlier stage, we should all be in a better place than where we are now.

In my view, an entirely convincing argument for Evans's acquittal was the incongruity of the two verdicts at the first trial. The prosecution of Ched Evans, as presented at both his first trial and the second, rested on the contention that his so-called 'victim' lacked the capacity to consent to engage in sexual activity; for the fact of intercourse was never disputed and the unnamed girl made no allegations but rather disclaimed all recollection not just of having intercourse with Evans but of the entire sequence of events which led to it. For this reason, even to call her a *complainant* – except in the most formal, legalistic sense – is grossly misleading. Moreover – as was pointed out at the retrial – the fact that a complainant does not recall an event does not imply that she did not consent to it – or even enjoy it – at the time.

Unless the prosecution could have established that the girl quickly became more intoxicated between the two instances of sexual congress, the prospect of convicting Evans for a second time must have been very remote indeed; unless, of course, at least ten members of the new jury had been so prepossessed by the demonization that Evans has suffered, and which the prosecuting counsel endeavoured to perpetuate, that they were willing to convict him despite the extreme paucity of the evidence against him. To its credit, the second jury served the interests of justice much better than the first one had done. Another guilty verdict would have been as perverse as the original one that sent Evans to prison: for as Clayton McDonald asked at the end of the first trial: "How can he be guilty if I'm not guilty?" This question has never been answered satisfactorily. I venture to affirm that it never could be.

At the first trial, Evans's co-defendant, Clayton McDonald, was acquitted of rape even though he had had intercourse with the girl only a few minutes earlier. The glaring incongruity of the two verdicts always struck intelligent observers as bizarre, and it should have constituted immediate grounds for a successful appeal. As already observed (p. 49), Judges of Appeal are extremely reluctant to say: 'On this occasion the jury was wrong. The case needs to be re-examined.' Given the toxic climate of the times, it is possible that the early appeal judges felt under pressure to uphold the guilty verdict, even though it was highly dubious. The obdurate refusal to acknowledge the perversity of the original verdict meant that Ched Evans spent two and half years in prison for a crime he did not commit and – because of the duplicity, opportunism and moral cowardice of other individuals and corporate bodies – almost two more years in professional limbo before Chesterfield FC had the courage to sign him. Belatedly, justice was secured – but only because great pains were taken and substantial expense incurred to uncover new evidence. The acknowledgement of this new evidence by the Court of Appeal provided a fig leaf to mask – albeit incompletely – the disgrace of what had gone before. For nothing could adequately compensate for the wrong that Evans has suffered or atone for the years of stress and misery endured by those who love him.

In recent years, many of our national institutions have become the objects of cynical scrutiny. Large banks, some of which were once our greatest Building Societies, have been ruined by the greed and venality of their directors. Never in living memory have politicians been more mistrusted – a fact attested in part by the outcome of the 2016 EU Referendum. Sometimes people working in the education system, the health service, the churches, and the media fail to live up to the standards that were once expected of them. Though the prospect is a frightening one, it is quite conceivable that even the administration of justice may become tainted by ineptitude or corruption. As frequent news reports testify, and as is made evident by the commissioning of public enquiries into egregious incompetence and scandalous abuses of power in high places, there is no absolute guarantee that those appointed to offices of trust will discharge their duties properly. Our only safeguard – albeit an imperfect one – is constant vigilance and the determination to expose and denounce evils when they are perpetrated. Such was my aim in writing this little book.

Valediction.

I have found my task as an author engaging and stimulating; and I hope I have done a competent job in vindicating the reputation of an unduly maligned young man. However, I have also found this work deeply depressing. It has enlivened my awareness that I live in a land where many agencies and the people who are paid to serve them fall well short of mediocrity, both intellectually and morally. These are the wimps and the villains.

The heroes are the dedicatees of this little book: Ched himself, who has been determined to acquit himself of the odious name of rapist and salvage as best he can his tarnished reputation. Also, of course, his partner Natasha Massey and her father Karl, without whose steadfast and unflinching support he might not have triumphed or even survived. I wish them well, and am gratified to note that in his early appearances on the pitch for Chesterfield, Ched performed admirably.

9. Remarks on Luke Gittos's book: *Why Rape Culture is a Dangerous Myth: from Steubenville to Ched Evans.*

Any book which confronts fashionable orthodoxies, challenges the tyranny of political correctness, and bestirs people to think anew about important issues deserves a welcome. So, having already made two references to it (pp. 4 & 17 above) I extend a welcome – albeit not an unqualified one – to this highly polemic monograph. In one way, the task that the author has set himself is a peculiar one; for, as he points out (pp. 88 & 90), since the term *rape culture* is a kind of shorthand for an agglomeration of social phenomena alleged to make rape more probable, then it is likely to be too wide in its denotation to be genuinely explanatory, and so vague as to elude the force of focussed criticism. *Rape culture* is in fact little more than a slogan.

Chapter 1 is about statistics: how they can be deceptive and how they can be abused to mislead the unwary. Much of the data about allegations of rape must, from their very nature, involve an element of great uncertainty. They should therefore be interpreted with the uttermost circumspection. For instance, an increase in allegations does not necessarily imply an increase in the rate of the crime. I have already endorsed the author's assault on the target-driven culture of the Crown Prosecution Service (Gittos, 18, 30-2, 62-3), conflicting, as it does, with the detachment and objectivity with which prosecutors should make their decisions.

In Chapters 2 and 3 he writes from an avowedly libertarian perspective. He clearly deplores what he considers to be the gratuitous interference by the state and its institutions to effect 'the regulation of intimacy' (a recurring theme, not defined until the final pages). However, in my view he overstates the extent of this intervention and fails to appreciate why – as some would argue – it might sometimes be justified. He welcomes the weakening of the moral restraints which until the mid-20th century regulated to some degree most people's lives (38-9). The erosion of conventional morality has certainly empowered people to make choices more freely; but in so doing it has enabled them to make *bad* choices as often as good ones: to such a degree that some people's lives are now so ill-conducted that they frequently stand in need of professional, magisterial, or judicial intervention. State interference is – arguably – a necessary attempt to cure the ills that personal self-restraint might once have forestalled.

Indeed, the book is underlain by the sanguine Rousseau-like assumption – unstated but clearly implied – that human beings can somehow thrive without the influence of either social convention or the law. Gittos too readily dismisses the possibility that people are formed – for better or worse – by the culture and institutions in which they grow up. From the time of Moses, or possibly longer, older and wiser heads have known that human nature is readily susceptible to corruption and therefore needs to be placed under restraints.

Chapter 3 is an account of how since the turn of the century the law has been amended to facilitate the prosecution of alleged rape and to make securing convictions easier, even in circumstances where this might be unsafe. As the author contends, such changes render implausible – or even fatuous – any claim that our society views rape with indifference.

Chapter 4 is entitled 'The Impact of the Rape Panic'. Here, to my great surprise, Gittos disclaims any sympathy for the plight of Ched Evans, declaring: '*Personally, I do not find the fact of Evans's conviction particularly troubling…* [and] *I am not overly troubled by the fact that he received a lengthy prison sentence.*' (94) When it comes to the details of this case, he is on very weak ground indeed. Within two pages (94-5) there are *four* factual inaccuracies: (i) Evans was released from prison not in August 2014 but in October; (ii) the on-line petition to blight his prospects of reinstatement at Sheffield United was launched not *after* his release, but six months earlier; (iii) the petition attracted not 'in excess of 60,000 signatures' but about 170,000 mouse-clicking acts; and – most seriously of all – (iv) he intimates that Evans was guilty of 'sexual violence', although there was no evidence that either Evans or his co-defendant deployed force or violence of any kind whatsoever.

Also to my surprise, Gittos does not comment on the perversity of the disparate verdicts in this case: the fact that while Evans was convicted, his co-accused, who had had intercourse with the girl only minutes earlier, was acquitted. Indeed, his cavalier attitude to Evans is utterly incongruous with the general tenor of the book and in stark contrast to his concern for the plight of drunken students: *'Should we really lock up students who have regrettably drunken flings with one another?'* (77). It seems that there is to be one law for students and another for footballers: an Orwellian instance, perhaps, where some animals are to be deemed more equal than others! To his credit, Gittos deplores the unrelenting campaign after Evans's release from prison to prevent his return to professional football, which he rightly regards as an attempt to impose extra-judicial punishment.

I suspect that the inclusion of Evans's name in the book's subtitle was in part a marketing ploy, as was the inclusion of the name *Steubenville* – a town in Ohio where in August 2012 there was a notorious case of multiple rape involving students at a local high school. I agree with this author that one effect of recent developments has been particularly unfortunate: namely that many more young people probably see others as potentially threatening to a degree that would not have been the case a generation or more ago (101-6). The social climate is now poisoned by suspicion and mistrust. However, Gittos seems reluctant to acknowledge that areas of such great personal intimacy as sexual and amorous encounters are indeed areas of potential vulnerability. This is why they need to be negotiated with great delicacy if human beings are not to become brutalised and degraded.

My reservations notwithstanding, this book should be welcomed as a vigorous contribution to an important debate that no pressure group or vested interest should be allowed to stifle.

Bibliography of Works Cited or Mentioned.

Dates in square brackets refer to the year of first publication where this is different from that of the edition cited.

Baldwin, Alec (with Tabb, Mark): *A Promise to Ourselves – A Journey through Fatherhood and Divorce* (New York: St Martin's Press, 2008)

Butler, Joseph: *Fifteen Sermons Preached at the Rolls Chapel* [1726] Edited by the Very Rev. W.R. Matthews (London: G. Bell & Sons Ltd, 1967)

Clifford, William Kingdon: *Lectures and Essays*, edited by Leslie Stephen & Frederick Pollock. 2 vols. (London: Macmillan & Co., 1879)

Cross, F.L. (editor): *The Oxford Dictionary of the Christian Church* (London: Oxford University Press, 1958)

Dennis, John: *Vice and Luxury Publick Mischiefs* (London: W. Mears, 1724) Included in Stafford (1997). See below.

Diorio, Joseph A: Entry on Catherine MacKinnon in *Sex from Plato to Paglia*. See below under Soble, Alan.

Gittos, Luke: *Why Rape Culture is a Dangerous Myth*. (Exeter: Societas / Imprint Academic, 2015)

Horace [Quintus Horatius Flaccus]: *Odes.* Latin text and English translation by Niall Rudd. 'Loeb Classical Library' No.33 (Cambridge Mass. & London: Harvard University Press, 2004)

Hume, David: *Enquiries concerning Human Understanding and concerning the Principles of Morals* [1748 & 1751] edited by L.A. Selby-Bigge and revised by P.H. Nidditch (Oxford: Clarendon Press, 1975)

----- *A Treatise of Human Nature* [1739-40] edited by David Fate Norton & Mary Norton (Oxford University Press, 2000)

Mandeville, Bernard: *The Fable of the Bees* [1714 & 1729] edited by F.B. Kaye, 2 vols. (Oxford: Clarendon Press, 1924) Reprinted many times.

----- *A Modest Defence of Publick Stews: or, An Essay upon Whoring...* (London: A. Moore, 1724) Edited by Irwin Primer (New York: Palgrave Macmillan, 2006)
----- *A Letter to Dion…* (London: J Roberts, 1732) Included in Stafford, 1997. See below.
Mao Tse-Tung: *Quotations from Chairman Mao* (Peking [now known as Beijing]: Foreign Language Press, 1966)
Pope, Alexander: *The Poems of…* edited by John Butt (London: Methuen & Co. Ltd, 1963)
Smith, Adam: *The Theory of Moral Sentiments* [1759] edited by D.D. Raphael and A.L. Macfie (Oxford: Clarendon Press, 1976)
Soble, Alan (editor): *Sex from Plato to Paglia – A Philosophical Encyclopedia*, 2 vols. (Westport, CT: Greenwood Press, 2006)
Spencer, Herbert: *Social Statics* (London: John Chapman, 1851)
----- *Education: Intellectual, Moral, and Physical* (London: G. Manwaring, 1861) Subsequent editions were published by Williams & Norgate.
Stafford, J. Martin: 'Love and Lust Revisited: Intentionality, Homosexuality and Moral Education' *Journal of Applied Philosophy* Vol. 5, No. 1, (1988) 87-100.
----- 'The Two Minds of Roger Scruton' *Studies in Philosophy and Education* Vol. 11, No. 2 (1991) 187-193.
Both the above are reprinted in:
----- *Essays on Sexuality and Ethics* (Solihull: Ismeron, 1995)
----- (as editor) *Private Vices, Publick Benefits? The Contemporary Reception of Bernard Mandeville* (Solihull: Ismeron, 1997)
----- Entries in *Sex from Plato to Paglia*. See above under Soble.
----- *The Prosecutor Unmask'd – Four Dialogues occasioned by the Prosecution of Michael Le Vell.* (Solihull: Ismeron, 2014)
Stewart, Dugald: *The Philosophy of the Active and Moral Powers of Man*, 2 vols. [1828]. Included as Volumes VI and VII in *Collected Works...* edited by Sir William Hamilton, 11 volumes, (Edinburgh: Thomas Constable & Co., 1854-60)